To

_____

From

_____

Date

_____

Shouts of Joy: Celebrations for the Fearless, Faithful Heart
Copyright © 2017 by DaySpring
Print ISBN 978-1-68408-115-8
Manuscript written by Patricia Mitchell in association with Snapdragon Editorial
Group℠, Tulsa, Oklahoma.

Published by DaySpring
P. O. Box 1010
Siloam Springs, AR 72761

Quotations marked KJV are taken from the King James Version. Public Domain.

Quotations marked NLT are taken from the Holy Bible, New Living Translation,
copyright © 1996, 2004, 2015 by Tyndale House Foundation. Used by permission of
Tyndale House Publishers Inc., Carol Stream, Illinois 60188. All rights reserved.

Quotations marked CEV are taken from the Contemporary English Version.
Copyright © 1995 by American Bible Society.

Quotations marked GNT are taken from the Good News Translation. Copyright ©
1992 by the American Bible Society.

Quotations marked NASB are taken from the New American Standard Bible.
Copyright © 1960, 1962, 1963, 1968, 1971, 1972, 1973, 1975, 1977, 1995 by The Lockman
Foundation, La Habra, CA 90631 90631. All rights reserved.

Quotations marked TLB are taken from The Living Bible. Copyright © 1971 by
Tyndale House Foundation. Used by permission of Tyndale House Publishers Inc.,
Carol Stream, Illinois 60188. All rights reserved.

Quotations marked THE MESSAGE are taken from The Message. Copyright © 1993,
1994, 1995, 1996, 2000, 2001, 2002 by Eugene H. Peterson.

Quotations marked NCV are taken from The Holy Bible, New Century Version®.
Copyright © 2005 by Thomas Nelson, Inc.

Quotations marked HCSB are taken from the Holman Christian Standard Bible.
Copyright © 1999, 2000, 2002, 2003, 2009 by Holman Bible Publishers, Nashville,
Tennessee. All rights reserved.

Quotations marked NRSV are taken from the New Revised Standard Version Bible.
Copyright © 1989 the Division of Christian Education of the National Council of the
Churches of Christ in the United States of America. Used by permission. All rights
reserved.

Quotations marked NKJV are taken from the New King James Version®. Copyright ©
1982 by Thomas Nelson. Used by permission. All rights reserved.

Printed in China

SHOUTS OF *Joy*

Celebrations for the Fearless, Faithful Heart

PATRICIA MITCHELL

Table of Contents

Introduction

     Earthly fathers work hard to provide for their children, ensuring that they have all they need in the way of food, clothing, education, health care, and a safe place to live. But it doesn't end there. For most fathers, just enough is not nearly enough. They go to great lengths to shower their children with benefits designed to induce smiles and other expressions of joy. In the same way, our heavenly Father enjoys lavishing blessing after blessing on His children and listening to their shouts of joy.

     This book is designed to encourage strong expressions of joy and praise to God from those who call Him Father. As you read, allow yourself to revel in His kindness, goodness, and love. Take each gift to heart and follow it with shouts of joy and thankfulness. He is a great and mighty God, the magnificent Creator of everything, and yet, He chooses not to be aloof and uninvolved in our lives. His desire is for you to know Him as He knows you. He wants to provide you with all you need, and He wants to see you smile and express your joy for all He has given you.

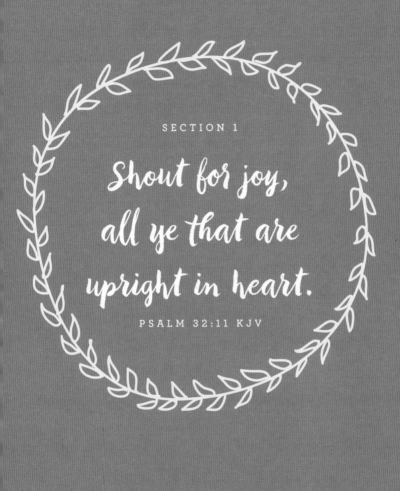

SECTION 1

Shout for joy,
all ye that are
upright in heart.

PSALM 32:11 KJV

The Ultimate Artist

God looked over all that he had made,
and it was excellent in every way.

GENESIS 1:31 TLB

To truly understand the heart of an artist, you need to study his work. Sit still and examine his brush strokes. Note his favorite color palette. Consider his subject matter. Compare his masterpieces with those of other artists.

God is the ultimate artist. His creations are so amazing that a lifetime is not long enough to fully appreciate them. Even the simplest butterfly shows His creativity, attention to detail, and love of beauty. A spectacular sunset affirms His brilliant sense of color and design. No other artist, no matter how gifted, can begin to match the quality of His work.

Now consider this. You are one of God's most cherished creations. Of course, no one on this earth is perfect. None of us measure up to the original version of us, lovingly crafted in His workshop at the beginning of time. If you were able to see the original you, however, you might be surprised to note that what you consider your greatest flaws of face and form are instead unique details of His artistic genius. There is no arguing with a true artist!

*It isn't that God lies
to Himself about us.
It's just that He sees us
as He created us to be.*

ANGELA DUNHAM

Shout Out

Today, I will see myself with new eyes!

The Great Race

Let us run the race before us and never give up.
HEBREWS 12:1 NCV

From sprints to marathons, committed runners tell us that there are keys to running a great race. Stay in shape. Stay alert. Pace yourself. Keep your eyes on the goal. And of course, never give up.

Life can feel like a race at times. It's easy to get tired and discouraged when you encounter obstacles or find yourself eating the asphalt. Still the rules of any great race apply. Stay in good spiritual shape. Stay alert to God's voice in your heart. Pace yourself; burn out is a reality. Keep your eyes on your heavenly Father; relationship with Him is the goal of every well-run life. And resist the urge to give up and miss out on the greatest victory of all.

The race God has designed specifically for you won't be a walk in the park. In fact, it will push you to your limit—or your full potential if you can begin to think of it that way. But you won't be running alone. God will be there to support you, give you strength and endurance, and cheer you on every step of the way.

*For the Christian running
the race of life,
God is his sponsor,
his sideline encourager,
as well as his prize
for staying the course.*

BECKY SAMSON

Shout Out

Watch out world! I'm coming through!

The Priceless Gift of Purpose

We know that God causes all things
to work together for good to those who love God,
to those who are called according to His purpose.

ROMANS 8:28 NASB

A sense of purpose is key to happiness. Although specifics change as you enter each life stage, gain experience, and meet current circumstances, the hallmarks of purpose remain the same. It's the activity that captures your heart and keeps you engaged and satisfied. It's the niche you so gladly fill, reminding you that God put you here for a reason. It's what gets you up in the morning!

Maybe you knew from an early age what you wanted to do in life, you pursued it, and you take great satisfaction in it. Then again, maybe your purpose was, or still is, less well-defined. Keep your eyes open, because it's there! A clear sense of purpose can come with the sudden awareness that you're at this time, this place, and it's not by chance. Your purpose may dawn on you gradually in the course of living a seemingly ordinary life. Basically, you're fulfilled. Satisfied. Happy! You possess the priceless gift of purpose.

God creates no one without a reason. If you already know what that reason is, woo-hoo! If you can't see it, look again. Ask your creator to open your eyes to His good and godly purpose for you.

God sees every one of us;
He creates each soul...
for a purpose.

JOHN HENRY NEWMAN

Shout Out

I am here for a God-given purpose!

Season to Taste

Choose life, that you and your offspring may live.
DEUTERONOMY 30:19 ESV

First the ingredients list, then the cooking instructions, and finally the note: Season to taste. You've got all the must-haves to make the recipe, all the know-how you need to proceed, but the choice of seasoning is up to you. It's personal, neither good nor bad. It's simply what tickles your taste buds.

In your life, there are circumstances you cannot change, like the ingredients you've been given. The instructions are laid out in God's Word. And then there are those important choices you can make that season your days to taste—God's taste and yours too. For example, your option to liberally sprinkle your thoughts, words, and actions with the fragrant seasoning of kindness and thoughtfulness. Your decision to add a dash of fun to routine days by maintaining an upbeat attitude and keeping a smile on your lips. Your prayer to God for a spirit sweetened through and through with faith, trust, and love.

You have been given the ingredients, and God has supplied all the necessary instructions. Now here's where you get to choose: Season to taste!

Circumstances and situations do color life, but you have been given the mind to choose what the color shall be.

JOHN HOMER MILLER

Shout Out

I choose to season my life with kindness and love!

Zest for Life

*Don't burn out; keep yourselves
fueled and aflame.*

ROMANS 12:11 THE MESSAGE

Most kids are naturally interested, curious, and discovery-focused. They delight in learning new facts about the world, expanding their knowledge, and advancing their abilities. When they master a skill, whether simple or advanced, they beam with earned pride. Kids have enthusiasm to spare!

As years pass, however, all too often, enthusiasm fades. It gets undermined by worry and anxiety. It gets buried under a blasé façade, a seen-it-all air designed to convey urbanity and sophistication. But did you know that a vibrant, lively, and living relationship with God is fueled by enthusiasm? An enthusiastic acceptance of His good will for you. An enthusiastic desire to build and strengthen your relationship with Him. An enthusiastic embrace of your life, every new day.

Re-energize your enthusiasm for God and godliness. Take a cue from kids: explore, discover, learn, create. Join a Bible study to further explore Scripture and its application to your life. Spend time outdoors, appreciating the beauty of God's creation. Most of all, surround yourself with enthusiastic people (especially kids), because enthusiasm is delightfully contagious. Catch it, and pass it on!

*Every great and commanding
movement in the annals
of history is the triumph
of enthusiasm.*

RALPH WALDO EMERSON

Shout Out

*I'm bursting with excitement
about my God!*

Is It True?

Every word of God proves true.
PROVERBS 30:5 TLB

Social media overflows with stories. While some may spark a memory, make you laugh, or draw a tear, others can leave you scared silly. Then it's time to ask yourself: *How do I know this is true?* Perhaps you'll visit an authoritative website, or check in with someone who can speak knowledgeably on the topic. Why take something seriously that isn't true?

The Bible's stories can uplift and encourage, renew and restore, comfort and soothe. No problem, right? But they can also challenge, frighten, mystify, perplex, confuse, repel, and shock. You read and wonder: *Is this true?* How do you know the Bible's words, especially the difficult and controversial teachings, apply in today's world, and most importantly, to you? The answer matters, because Scripture either does or does not get its place as your go-to source of God's wise counsel, spiritual nourishment, and day-to-day reassurance.

Don't be afraid to ask questions. Often further reading and reflection will open the truth to you. An informed, Bible-savvy friend or counselor can help. Events from your own life story might highlight the truth and relevance of God's good Word. Don't wonder. God wants you to know the truth—all of it.

There is nothing so powerful as truth.

DANIEL WEBSTER

Shout Out

When I'm in doubt, I check it out!

Root of the Matter

As a garden enables what is sown to spring up,
so the Lord God will cause righteousness
and praise to spring up.

ISAIAH 61:11 HCSB

For every thriving flower garden, there's a busy gardener. Perhaps several! For without their dedication and patience and their effort and know-how, weeds quickly chock out lush blossoms. Without their willingness to prune and nurture prized plants and vines, healthy stalks soon become weak and withered.

Your spiritual life and the flower garden share several things in common. First, they both need ongoing care and attention. Yes, God has planted seeds of faith in your heart, but He invites you to nurture them with daily Scripture reading, spiritual reflection, and heartfelt prayer. Second, negligence allows weeds, such as materialism, addiction, and selfishness, to suffocate the roots of faith. Once spiritual weeds get established, your relationship with God is easily overrun.

Third, a skillful gardener knows how to protect tender seedlings, prop up weak branches, dig out noxious growths, and prune blooming plants so they yield bigger, brighter, and healthier blossoms. Your gardener is God. Ask Him to send His Spirit into the garden of your heart. Let Him get you to the root of a life resplendent with luscious, fragrant flowers to possess, and also to give away!

*There are no shortcuts
to spiritual maturity.
It takes time to be holy.*

ERWIN W. LUTHER

Shout Out

I am here for a God-given purpose!

Light for the Way

*I know the plans I have for you, says the Lord.
They are plans for good and not for evil,
to give you a future and a hope.*

JEREMIAH 29:11 TLB

When driving at night, especially on a rural road, you can see no farther than your headlights allow. Instinctively you slow down and remain especially cautious, because your visibility is extremely limited.

In a similar way, you cannot know for certain what lies in the years ahead. Despite creating even the most well-thought-out plan for your future, you just never know what's around the next corner. Even though your expectations are reasonable, events and circumstances can pop up that you could never anticipate. However, you can be prepared for this if you're relying on God's ability to define the future, rather than your own.

Does this mean the dreams and goals you have for your life don't count? Of course not. It just means that they're subject to God's will and His good plans for you. His vision extends to all eternity! He knows every bump, twist, turn, and dip in the road. He can light each blind curve and take you through every looming shadow that crosses your path. When it's too dark to see ahead, slow down, and let God navigate. Let Him show you the way, inch by inch, mile by mile.

*He begs you to
leave the future to him,
and mind the present.*

GEORGE MCDONALD

Shout Out

I'm planning to leave the driving to God!

The Best Kitchen

God uses us to make the knowledge about Christ
spread everywhere like a sweet fragrance.
2 CORINTHIANS 2:14 GNT

Imagine the aroma of cinnamon buns filled with raisins baking in the oven, cookies liberally sprinkled with chocolate chips warm and ready to eat, or a savory stew loaded with meat, potatoes, and vegetables just off the stove. Without doubt, the cook in this kitchen doesn't scrimp on ingredients! Your nose tells you. And your eyes. And your taste buds will shout it out loud!

As you grow in God, your thoughts, words, and actions take on the fragrance of goodness and kindness, wisdom and discernment. Others begin to see something about you that delights their eyes, like your attentiveness to their needs and your consideration of their feelings. Through you, they taste the sweetness of what it means to follow God in real and practical ways. And then they ask about the ingredients—what makes you so attractively different, so delightfully refreshing. What makes you "you"?

His Spirit is working in the "kitchen" of your heart. He uses only the best ingredients, and He never scrimps. Living with Him is like the banquet of a lifetime, with plenty of goodness to share!

What you are is God's gift to you.
What you make of yourself
is your gift to him.

AUTHOR UNKNOWN

Shout Out

Fill me with Your good food forever!

Be True to You

Body and soul, I am marvelously made!
I worship in adoration—what a creation!
PSALM 139:15 GNT

Although you may share many hopes, dreams, values, and ideals with others, you are still an individual. No one, not even an identical twin, possesses exactly the same blend of traits and characteristics, talents and capabilities. Even though you might go through the same situation as many other people, you will emerge with your personal perspective based on your outlook, personality, beliefs, temperament, and experiences.

Treasure you, rejoice in you, because God created you "you," not a clone of someone else. Value yourself, your thoughts, and your ideas. Start wherever you are right now. Build on your abilities, follow your interests, and, as much as possible, do what brings you heartfelt joy and will result in lasting happiness.

Will being true to you result in rounds of applause from others? Maybe not, particularly if someone wants you to fill a predetermined, convenient-for-them role. But what you're sure to hear is a round of applause from yourself. And it's easy to imagine the high-fives that happen in heaven when a child of God decides to become the unique, joyful, and marvelous person God created!

*Every human being is intended
to have a character of his own;
to be what no others are;
and to do what no other can do.*

WILLIAM ELLERY CHANNING

Shout Out

I am me and no other!

Real Life Dreams

Be transformed by the renewing of your mind,
so that you may discern what is the good,
pleasing, and perfect will of God.

ROMANS 12:2 HCSB

It's a popular notion these days that individuals can accomplish whatever they can dream, or achieve anything they can imagine. In some ways, it's true. Perseverance over time yields amazing results, and people with drive and a vision often do what others claim is impossible.

But in other ways, it's false. Everyone has limitations, even super-achievers. Each of us is born with physical, intellectual, and emotional boundaries that cannot be crossed successfully. Quite often, there are also overwhelming circumstances that inhibit free movement and expression, as well as deeply held life-values that mean more than our own personal dream-chasing. Not everyone can or does decide to go after their dream.

If you're feeling frustrated with your progress, or if you have a dream that may not seem to be taking shape in any real way, turn to the one who created you. He gave you your specific talents and abilities, and He meant for you to use them for a real purpose in a real world. Ask about His dream for you, because it's the one that can and will come true, and perhaps in unimaginable and truly amazing ways.

A dream that comes true
and brings beauty and life
must come from
the heart of God.

C. E. HOLLIS

Shout Out

I want to dream God's amazing
dreams for me!

The Upside of Uh-Oh!

If someone is caught in any wrongdoing,
you who are spiritual should restore
such a person with a gentle spirit.

GALATIANS 6:1 HCSB

A gracious host lets slip a tactless remark. A savvy company manager makes the worst possible business decision. A good friend fails to notice her best friend's need. No matter how capable and competent we are, we mess up from time to time!

Mistakes are embarrassing, and they bring us down a peg or two. But here's the upside. For starters, we're reminded that we're human, just like everyone else. And then we're compelled to ask forgiveness from God, as well as from those who may have been hurt by our words or actions. Finally, we're motivated never to do it again. We're committed to learn from what happened, grow beyond it, and avoid the same blunder next time.

When you stumble, the worst thing you can do is stay down. Remember who you are—a beloved, but human, child of your heavenly Father. He has promised to come to your aid, comfort you, and bring peace to your heart and mind. You can rely on His pardon. You can ask forgiveness of others. You can let your "bads" serve not only as a lesson for you but also as a good example of how to handle them.

*The man who does things
makes many mistakes,
but he never makes the biggest
mistake of all—doing nothing.*

BENJAMIN FRANKLIN

Shout Out

*I make a habit of learning
from my mistakes!*

Compassion in Action

*God's chosen ones, holy and loved, put on
heartfelt compassion, kindness, humility,
gentleness, and patience.*
COLOSSIANS 3:12 HCSB

Thanks to awesome technological advances, we get to watch events unfold around the globe with the click of a button! But even casual observers of national and global happenings can find themselves overwhelmed by bad news. Conflicts and wars. Hardships and sorrows. Natural disasters. We feel powerless to help, and soon the words and pictures lose their power to move us. It's called compassion fatigue.

Compassion starts snoring when it's left dozing inside your heart and mind. Although you may not possess the resources to donate millions or travel to far-flung places, you can counter bad news with good news. The smallest kindness you actually do for one person near you means more than the deepest emotion you can pour out for the world's population. The practical help you might give a neighbor lifts a burden, while trying to sort through the legitimacy of international charities adds a burden. Small, consistent contributions work, but grand wish-I-coulds don't. Compassion-in-action works, and helps you get rid of compassion fatigue.

Do you feel for those who are needy, sick, hungry, lonely, or desperate? Jesus did. But He didn't stop with a feeling. He helped one at a time, right where He was.

Because I cannot do everything
I will not refuse to do the
something that I can do.

EDWARD EVERETT HALE

Shout Out
I can make a compassionate difference right where I am!

Walk with God

*God's kingdom is about pleasing God,
about living in peace, and about true happiness.*
ROMANS 14:17 CEV

What would make you happy? Many imagine that being free to take it easy, do their own thing, and go wherever their whims and interests lead them would be just the ticket. But ask anyone whose face reflects the soft smile of fulfillment and whose eyes glow with purpose and meaning. In other words, a happy person. You might get a different answer.

Probe their secret, and you're apt to hear about a life lived not for self, but for others, despite personal sacrifices. Dig deeper to learn about the strong faith that has seen them through difficulties and hardships, griefs and losses. You'll discover that happy, satisfied people are always engaged in pursuits higher than temporary pleasure and invested in quests beyond private gain. So much for doing your own thing!

Genuine happiness starts with deep and lasting values applied and practiced day by day. It develops as God's Spirit increases your faith and trust in His wisdom, even when times are tough or call for difficult choices. The result is happiness unattainable by any other means—the happiness of walking together with God.

Happiness is neither without us nor within us. It is in God, both without us and within us.

BLAISE PASCAL

Shout Out

I'm looking for real happiness!

Tactful Encounters

To make an apt answer is a joy to anyone,
and a word in season, how good it is!
PROVERBS 15:23 NRSV

Perhaps you know someone who's able to confront others with uncomfortable truths, yet can do so without demeaning them. This is the parent, pastor, teacher, supervisor, or friend whose tactfully worded correction or criticism leaves you thankful to have heard it and motivated to do better next time.

Tact is the ability to tell necessary truths in the kindest possible way. From pointing out a child's wrongdoing, to opening a difficult conversation with a dear friend or dealing with a noisy neighbor, tactful words get the message across without engendering anger or resentment. Tact allows you to speak to the point without deflating the person's self-esteem and treading on their dignity. It repairs relationships, encourages growth, inspires improvement, and builds mutual respect.

Remember that everyone you speak to is like yourself, someone deeply loved by God, so make prayer the prelude to any difficult conversation. Reflect on the specifics of what you want to say, and whether your insights will be helpful to the hearer. Then, ask God for the courage to speak in the most tactful, constructive, and loving way possible.

*Silence is not always tact
and it is tact that is golden,
not silence.*

SAMUEL BUTLER

Shout Out

*I will speak necessary truths
with kindness and tact.*

Forward Thinking

Though he give you the bread of adversity
and water of affliction,
yet he will be with you to teach you

ISAIAH 30:23 TLB

Suppose you can't walk a mile down the street. It stands to reason that you aren't able to run a marathon. If you've never bothered to master simple math, it's not likely you're up to passing a calculus test. And if you would rather quit than surmount life's small hurdles, how will you be able to overcome the big ones?

Adversity has been called God's training ground. The more willing you are to tackle ordinary setbacks, the more capable and self-confident you grow. Later, when complex problems arise (and they will) you're accustomed to saying, "Well, God helped me through back then, so He's not going to fail me now!" Such a bold statement of faith wouldn't occur to you unless you've been there, done that, and leaned on Him every step of the way.

When you fall, reach up. Put your hand in God's because He's willing and able to pull you up and get you going again. And this time you'll be walking with more street smarts than you had before. How did you handle your last stumble? Think about it. Chances are good you learned something that can move you forward today!

There is no education like adversity.

BENJAMIN DISRAELI

Shout Out

Each setback serves to push me forward!

Five-Star Day

*The payoff for meekness and Fear-of-God
is plenty and honor and a satisfying life.*
PROVERBS 22:4 THE MESSAGE

What does it take for you to give a day a five-star rating? Some would say being out among people, exchanging ideas, and collaborating on plans and projects. A noisy, laughter-filled space with plenty of pats on the back is a great day! Others would prefer working solo or in a small, close-knit group and quiet setting. Hours on end without interruptions? Ahhh! Perfect!

Recall your most recent five-star day. What made it that way? It's likely that the people (or lack of people) present, the project you were working on, and the atmosphere around you left you feeling renewed, energized, and satisfied. That evening, you didn't plop into bed exhausted. Instead you spent time mulling over everything you accomplished, talking about it with a friend or loved one, and thanking God for the gift and privilege of doing it.

A calendar full of five-star days adds up to a life of fulfillment. Perhaps there are changes you can make in how you spend your time or, most significantly, in how you perceive your present situation, that would add several more stars to upcoming day's ratings!

Fulfillment comes as a by-product of our love for God. And that satisfaction is better than we ever imagined.

ERWIN W. LUTZER

Shout Out

Today is going to be a five-star day!

Know the Answer

Thank God that, although you used to be slaves of sin, you obeyed from the heart that pattern of teaching you were transferred to.

ROMANS 6:17 HCSB

"Did you see *that?*" gasps a driver. "What's wrong?" says his passenger. As the driver points out the traffic maneuver he found blatantly illegal, the passenger looks increasingly puzzled. "Really? I thought that was perfectly okay!" So who's right? To find out, they checked the motor vehicle code, the authority on what's legal on the road, and what's not.

When it comes to matters of faith, conduct, and Christian knowledge, the authority is the Bible. The Bible makes God's will known to us, and His will does not change even if our opinion differs from His. Just as the driver and his passenger could argue for hours on the legality of the traffic maneuver, a definitive *yes* or *no* rested with the law of the road. We can debate issues of *right* and *wrong* all we want, but the true answer—the answer that won't change—lies in Scripture, the law—and love—of God.

The Bible's rules are designed to guide you safely through life. They reflect the love and wisdom of your heavenly Father, who wants to make your journey smart and joyful, allowing you to truly delight in the scenery along the way.

A Bible that is falling apart probably belongs to someone who isn't.

CHRISTIAN JOHNSON

Shout Out

I'll look to You, God, for answers!

Keep Growing!

*My prayer for you is that you will overflow
more and more with love for others,
and at the same time keep on growing
in spiritual knowledge and insight.*

PHILIPPIANS 1:9 TLB

Remember a time when you weren't, say, four years old but four-and-a-half? Not in fourth grade but *almost fifth*? Each birthday was cake-and-candle proof that you were older. Every grade ahead put you that much nearer to big-kid status. You were growing!

As adults, we drop the months from our age (and some of us might drop a few years, too). Graduation took place years ago. Yet, spiritually speaking, we have a lot of classes to take and growing yet to do. There's still room to grow in understanding, wisdom, and self-control. We haven't yet exhausted opportunities to explore, ponder, learn, discover, and appreciate God's will and His ways in our lives and in the world. The Scripture verse we've heard a hundred times before suddenly swells with meaning and significance. A seemingly random remark by another "student" deepens insight, broadens understanding, and leads to a whole fresh way of thinking and acting.

The school of spirituality is open to all ages. Classes are available year-round. Keep your enrollment current, and, most of all, keep growing in the knowledge and love of God.

*A vessel that grows
as it is filled will never be full.
The soul is like that.*

MEISTER ECKHART

Shout Out

Taking attendance? I'm here!

Self-Talk

Be an example to the believers with your words,
your actions, your love, your faith,
and your pure life.

1 TIMOTHY 4:12 NCV

If you want to keep your friends, you're not likely to hurl hurtful words at them, dismiss their opinions out of hand, or ride roughshod over their feelings. Yet when it comes to the closest friend you have—yourself—are you just as careful and considerate? Name-calling hurts others, and when you call yourself names, it hurts you.

Just as when you're talking with other people, constructive criticism you aim at yourself spurs positive change. A clear-eyed and rational assessment of what went wrong leads you to realistic, practical steps you can take toward improvement. Lesson learned? God's forgiveness prayerfully requested and fully accepted? Now leave the incident behind. Congratulate you, because you're willing and able to take responsibility for your actions. As of today, you know a little bit more about how to navigate the world in accordance with God's good will.

Listen to the words you tell yourself. Are they kindly chosen, constructive, and godly phrases and expressions? Do they build up, cheer up, and lift up? Do they leave you feeling at peace with yourself and with the desire to honor and respect yourself as someone God loves? If so, keep talking!

*I have noticed that nothing
I **never** said ever did
me any harm*

BENJAMIN DISRAELI

Shout Out

*I will speak to myself with honor
and respect!*

Miracles All Around

Sing to him; sing praises to him.
Tell about all his miracles
PSALM 105:2 NCV

While we long to see, hear, and feel miracles all around us, we rarely do. But life is full of miracles—great and small.

Imagine a curtain hangs between you and the outside world. Whatever lies on your side of the curtain—your daily routine, immediate responsibilities, and personal ambitions—gets your attention. From the time you get up in the morning until you tuck yourself into bed at night, it captures your full and complete concentration. No surprise: It's easy to forget there's anything else out there, anything beyond your side of the curtain.

Consciously and deliberately set aside a few minutes each day to pull away all that separates you from the beauty, amazement, and heart-soaring joy of creation. As if for the first time, see clouds floating across the sky, flowers bending in the breeze, the face of a friend, your hand in the hand of another. Hear wind in the trees, rain on the roof, and the distant call of birds on the wing. Feel what it's like to hold a child, cuddle a pet, hug a loved one. Yes, the miracles of God's handiwork are all around us! Why not delight in them today?

*A man who could make one rose…
would be considered most
wonderful: yet God scatters
countless such flowers around us.*

MARTIN LUTHER

Shout Out

Nothing comes between me and miracles!

The Good Giver

Listen to counsel and accept discipline,
that you may be wise the rest of your days.

PROVERBS 19:20 NASB

Imagine for a moment: An artist dips her brush into paint on her palette. Just as she's about to apply the color to her canvas, the brush recoils and shouts, "No, you fool! This is the wrong color!" Silly? Sure. Yet when we refuse to accept what God has chosen for us, we're acting like the petulant paintbrush. With no knowledge of God's purpose, we insist on telling Him what's best for us.

Perhaps there's something in your life right now that you don't like. This isn't something harmful; it's just not your preference. You're unhappy with it, but complaining drags you down and ignoring reality doesn't make it go away. Try focusing on the circumstance, situation, or event and ask yourself if there is any reason God may have allowed it to become part of your life at this time. If you can't come up with anything good to say about it, ask Him! There might be something valuable to learn. It could be essential to your growth or a door to your future.

God, your good giver, knows what you need most. When the color is His choice, make it your choice, too.

When God sorts out the weather
and sends rain,
Why, rain's my choice.

JAMES WHITCOMB RILEY

Shout Out

Your choice, God, is my choice!

Behind the Scenes

From Him the whole body, fitted and
knit together by every supporting ligament,
promotes the growth of the body.

EPHESIANS 4:16 HCSB

Out of thousands of start-ups, only a few entrepreneurs strike it rich. Out of hundreds of staffers, only some make it to the corporate boardroom. Out of several candidates, only one gets the nod. No success story, however, is complete without mentioning the family members, friends, assistants, teachers, trainers, mentors, and coaches who helped along the way. Behind-the-scenes supporters are the unsung heroes of anyone's victory. So are they any less successful? Certainly not!

When you use your knowledge, skills, and resources to boost the advancement of others, you're more than likely to get their support in return. When you're generous with praise and congratulations when someone else wins, the applause will be all the louder for you. But what if landing the top spot doesn't matter to you? Then you've already won! You find satisfaction in contributing to a winning cause without looking for public acknowledgement. You enjoy boosting others up without needing to push yourself forward. You love being who you are and where you are.

Talk to God about His definition of success for you. Is it on the scene or behind the scenes? Let Him guide you to the place that wouldn't be the same without you there!

The measure of our success will be the measure of our ability to help others.

F. B. MEYER

Shout Out

Success is doing my best wherever I am!

Glory Days

Don't throw away your confidence,
which has a great reward.
HEBREWS 10:35 HCSB

One constant throughout life is the naysayers. It could be someone close to you who, often with good intentions, insists on warning you of every conceivable pothole down the road. Or it might be the on-screen pundit who paints your entire generation with negative traits and characteristics. And by the way, do you know that the glory days ended twenty years ago?

Whatever your word for "poppycock" is, say it now. Which younger generation has lived exactly the same life as its elders, or has wanted to? In today's ever-changing society, it's next to impossible. Sure, there are challenges specific to one age group as opposed to another, but there are unique rewards, too. While hardships (whatever they may be) test resilience and endurance, advantages offer a way not only to manage difficulties but also advance through them. True, you do not know everything your elders know. Listen to them, because their experience might come in handy later on. But remember, what you know counts, too.

God has your yesterday, today, and tomorrow in His hand, just as He does for everyone, young and old. Be confident in your generation, and most of all, in yourself. The glory days are yours!

Seeing that distance and distrust
will do nothing for you,
try what drawing near
and confidence will do.

HORATIUS BONAR

Shout Out

I have what it takes to make it happen!

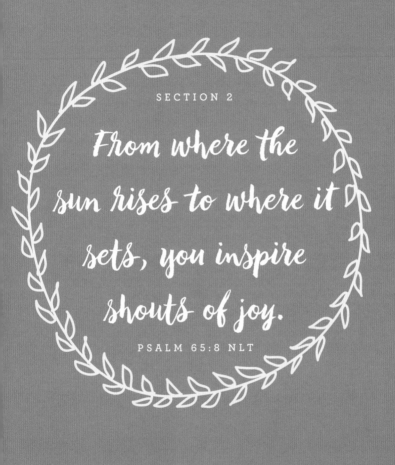

SECTION 2

From where the sun rises to where it sets, you inspire shouts of joy.

PSALM 65:8 NLT

Loved and Loving

He heals the brokenhearted
and binds up their wounds.
PSALM 147:3 NKJV

For broken hearts, love rarely returns easily. Protective layers of distrust, wariness, and suspicion form around it, shielding its tender center from further pain and hurt. Just as a scab develops over a wound, the heart's covering allows it to heal in its own time.

It could have been the passing of a loved one, the breakdown of a relationship, the betrayal of a friend. Perhaps the death of a beloved pet, the loss of a career, the ending of a dream, the memory of what once was. All hearts mourn, and not one of us can fully measure the depth of another's sorrow. Yet, as with wounds of the body, wounds of the heart are meant to heal. And God, the Great Physician, is the one whose comfort and consolation makes healing possible.

Thank God for all that love gave you and the memories it brought you. And then open your heart again. Let the gentle affection of another person, the pleading eyes of a furry friend, the lure of a new interest or intriguing idea capture your attention. Give yourself the God-created gift of loving and being loved in return.

*Loving, like prayer, is a power
as well as a process.
It is curative. It is creative.*

ZONA GALE

Shout Out

I am loved, and I choose to love again!

The Sound of Your Voice

Early in the morning before the sun is up,
I am praying and pointing out
how much I trust in you

PSALM 119:147 TLB

A close relationship between two people thrives on communication. Without sharing day-to-day happenings, thoughts, and observations, they understand less about each other. Eventually, they get out of the habit of talking together, and the relationship deteriorates. The same can be said about your relationship with God. Communication is crucial, and that's why He invites you to communicate with Him daily.

God longs for an ongoing, strong, and growing connection with you, and that's possible only if you speak to Him and learn from Him daily. When you're in the habit of expressing your feelings and desires to Him, you're acknowledging that He cares about you and He's the giver of all good things. Day by day, your heart and soul open to His presence. You're able to listen to His words with heightened attention and understanding. You're eager to apply His guidelines to your life, because you come to appreciate more and more the value of His timeless wisdom and unchangeable truths.

Keep the relationship between you and God thriving. Talk to Him every day and throughout the day. He loves to hear the sound of your voice.

Speak as naturally and as easily as you would to a friend, as God is just that.

JOHN B. COBURN

Shout Out

God, hear my prayer!

Butterfly Business

*It is God who works in you both to will
and to do for His good pleasure.*
PHILIPPIANS 2:13 NKJV

From a small, plain, and seemingly lifeless chrysalis emerges a bright, delicate, fluttering creature. Designed and created by our heavenly Father, the butterfly symbolizes His gift of renewal and resurrection, hope and transformation.

At times in your spiritual life, you might feel trapped by layers of inertia, sluggishness, and God-silence. There's been little or no observable progress in conquering outside temptations or overcoming personal challenges. There's been no brilliant "aha!" moment of sudden clarity, certainty, and understanding in matters of the spirit, and no instant realization of God's presence in your life. The transformation you expected when you started on this journey has yet to take place. Is there something wrong? Not at all.

God, in His wisdom, chooses the way of the butterfly for spiritual growth to take place. Though largely unseen even by you, His Spirit is working within you to nurture your faith. In time—God's time—you will begin to discern glimmers of comprehension, and act on them. In time—God's time—you will emerge from your chrysalis strong and trusting enough to sail on the uplifting winds of faith, hope, and love.

Grow, dear friends, but grow,
I beseech you, in God's way,
which is the only true way.

HANNAH WHITALL SMITH

Shout Out
Today I will spread my wings of faith!

Promise Power

In him every one of God's promises is a "Yes."
2 CORINTHIANS 1:20 NRSV

Promises aren't meant to be broken, but let's face it, they often are. Though a promise may have been made with good intentions, human weaknesses can undermine our ability or willingness to keep it. Life-altering circumstances can drive a wedge between a promise and reality, and the promise becomes unsustainable.

As you listen to God speak in His Word, you hear Him make promise after promise. Examples: He promises He will never leave you. He promises forgiveness and salvation, joy of heart and peace of mind. He promises to guide you throughout your life and guard you against spiritual harm. These and others are big promises, and here's the clincher: They're made by an unchangeable God. That means neither His will nor His intentions shift over time. He controls events, not the other way around. He possesses the power to say what He will do and do what He says.

When God makes a promise to you, grab hold of it. Rely on it and apply it to your everyday thinking and decision-making. And when you are moved to promise God your love and faithfulness, add this prayer: "Grant me, Lord, strength enough, and love enough, to keep it."

God is the God of promise.
He keeps his word, even when
that seems impossible.

COLIN URQUHART

Shout Out

Empower me, dear God,
to keep my promises!

Faith That Shows

No one after lighting a lamp puts it under the bushel basket, but on the lampstand, and it gives light to all in the house.

MATTHEW 5:15 NRSV

As dusk gently melds earth and sky, a meadow shrouds itself in secrecy. Though you can hear chirps and callings of night creatures and see shadowy silhouettes moving through the grasses, you can't tell what they're doing or where they've come from. There's just not enough light.

While faith resides in the privacy of your heart, it becomes visible to others only in the light of what you do. If your day-to-day actions consistently differ from God's guidelines and commandments, others can't detect the faith you say you possess. Certainly faith is present because there's the desire to know God, but it's not strong enough to shine through the shadows of long-held habit and unquestioned conformity with worldly standards. As if veiled by nightfall, evidence of faith may be glimpsed from time to time, but not seen clearly.

How do your actions reflect your faith? Ask God to help you apply what you believe to the things you do. Talking to others about God is important, but back up your words with actions. Show them! Ask God to help you bring your faith out into the daylight by practicing it, applying it, and living it every day.

*All our actions take their hues
from the complexion
of the heart.*

W. T. BACON

Shout Out

What I do shows what I believe!

All He Has to Say

Happy are those whose sins are forgiven,
whose wrongs are pardoned.

PSALM 32:1 GNT

Who doesn't like to listen when God says He loves us? It's a comforting, reassuring, and uplifting message that falls sweetly on our ears. But there's more to hear, because there's also the not-so-sweet subject of sin. If we won't listen to it, however, we can never begin to appreciate the depth, breadth, and strength of God's love.

Though we've all done things we shouldn't have, we don't like to admit it. We'd prefer to ignore our faults, and carry a heavy load of guilt that eats away at our peace of mind and joy of life. Now notice what God says: Confront the sin! Name it—no euphemisms allowed. Then He says this: "I love you so much that I forgive you, so much that I forgive every sin you've ever committed—yes, even that one."

If you want to truly understand God's love, tell Him what burdens your heart. Empty yourself to Him, and let Him fill your ears with His words of complete forgiveness. Savor the depth, breadth, and strength of His love for you!

When Christ hung, and bled,
and died, it was God saying
to the world—I love you.

BILLY GRAHAM

Shout Out
Your love is stronger than anything
I have done!

Family Matters

You are now citizens together with God's people and members of the family of God.

EPHESIANS 2:19 GNT

We belong to a family, whether by birth or adoption or marriage or friendship, and it's there that we can relax and be ourselves. We have a name among these special people, and a place where we care for them as they care for us. Yet even if something happens and we find ourselves on the outside, one fact remains. We belong to God's family.

In the Bible, God reveals Himself to you as your heavenly Father, and the reference to kinship isn't mere sentiment. God knows how important it is for you to belong to a family, that's why He takes His place as the head and foundation of all families. As His beloved child, you belong to it by creation and remain an active, engaged member of it by faith. Within His family, you have an identity and a purpose. Through the ministry of the Holy Spirit in your heart and your fellow family members, your soul is nurtured and your hands and feet equipped to take on your work in the world.

Give thanks for the family given to you by birth, circumstance, or life stage. And don't forget to mention your God-given family—His.

God's children form a large and happy family—learning and loving and each bearing the family likeness.

JESSICA BRINKER

Shout Out
I am one of His!

Let Bees Be Bees

You let me rest in fields of green grass.
You lead me to streams of peaceful water.
PSALM 23:2 CEV

It's a hive of activity! Though the frenetic busyness of bees swirling in and around their hive may produce something worthwhile—say, the honey you spread on your toast in the morning—your unrelenting busyness will not. Although you might feel dynamically active, at day's end there will be little to show for it except a very tired you.

A God-given rhythm governs your body, mind, and spirit. Your body craves rest, and you know whether you get your best rest by turning in early or by sleeping in late. Your mind, too, needs its time off. Consciously remove the bees, those ideas, anxieties, and worries whirling in your head. Allow yourself to consider nothing except the vast blueness of the sky, the cradling darkness of the night, and the infinite love of God for you. Set your spirit, your emotions, free to roam places invisible to the human eye, but where there's the sweetness of renewal and restoration.

Let bees be bees. God made them that way! But you are different. For you He made a place of deep peace and serenity, a place to leave the busyness of your day and find vital, life-giving rest for body, mind, and spirit.

First keep the peace within yourself, and then you can also bring peace to others.

THOMAS A. KEMPIS

Shout Out

Lord, I will rest at ease in You today!

How Rich Is God?

Your love is a treasure, and everyone finds
shelter in the shadow of your wings.
PSALM 36:7 CEV

Everything in the universe and beyond belongs to God. Just as He owns the stars above, He possesses the ores, minerals, and precious gems that lie deep below the surface of the earth. All this He created for us to discover, explore, use, admire, and appreciate.

But there's more to His wealth, and it goes way beyond material things, no matter how precious. That's His infinite love for each of us. Through the work of His Holy Spirit, He pours it out generously and lavishly. There's no limit to its height and depth! Need proof? Love compelled God to send His Son, Jesus, into our world to reveal exactly how strong and enduring His love is. Jesus' death on the cross for our sake shows God's willingness to stop at nothing to draw us close to Him. Jesus' resurrection from the grave demonstrates His power to renew, refresh, and restore us, all in the name of His great love.

Ask your fabulously wealthy God to fill you with the riches of His love. And when you do, open your arms and your heart to receive more than you can imagine, because you will. That's the kind of giver He is!

God is love,
he doesn't merely have it
or give it;
he gives himself—to all men,
to all sorts and conditions.

JOSEPH FLETCHER

Shout Out

Make me rich, Lord, in Your love!

Come As You Are

*If anyone thinks he is something
when he is nothing, he deceives himself.*

GALATIANS 6:3 NASB

You receive an invitation to a get-together with friends. You'll probably ask the host, "What can I bring?" Or you have your eye on a plum position at work, and you think to yourself: *What skills or experience do I have that I can bring to this job?* You want to arrive at the host's home with something in your hands, and at the interviewer's office with something on your résumé!

With God, it's different. He urges us to come with nothing in our hands. After all, what can we give Him that He hasn't Himself created? Don't bother to list your qualifications either. Anything you have accomplished is His gift to you rather than your gift to Him.

God invites you to approach Him free of anything that would come between the two of you, such as a claim of human worthiness, personal pride, or a sense of self-importance. Nor should you let fear, shame, or guilt keep you away. The emptier your hands and heart, the easier it is for you to receive His gifts of comfort and peace, forgiveness and love. Come, but bring nothing. Come as you are.

God says, "Come over here, child, and let me clean you up."
When we try to do it ourselves, we just make more work for Him.

HAZEL BISHOP WALTERS

Shout Out

Just as I am, I come to You!

Don't Worry!

*Which of you by worrying
can add a single hour to his life's span?*

LUKE 12:25 NASB

Worry is hard to avoid, because we're surrounded by things to worry about. Headlines scream of heartbreaking disasters, and social media buzz with frightening scenarios in the offing. We might find ourselves in desperate circumstances caused by events beyond our control or resulting from our own poor choices. Yet piercing through the thick wall of our daily concerns is God's clear and comforting voice saying, "Don't worry."

Though a useless platitude coming from the lips of a well-meaning friend, "don't worry" from God's Word is a powerful statement. It reaches out to you with the assurance that, no matter what is happening, He is still in control. Give Him your worries—all of them—and let Him strengthen you with the comfort of His presence. Hand over your feelings of hopelessness, and allow Him to renew your trust in His wisdom. Seek His guidance, and go where He leads.

Listen to God's "don't worry," because these aren't just nice-sounding words. They're backed by His powerful promise enough strength to carry you through and His willingness to stay by your side every step of the way.

*Worry never robs tomorrow
of its sorrow,
it only saps today
of its strength.*

ARCHIBALD JOSEPH CRONIN

Shout Out

I place my trust in God!

Weather Forecast

Parched ground that soaks up the rain and then produces an abundance of carrots and corn for its gardener gets God's "Well done!"
HEBREWS 6:7 THE MESSAGE

When it rains outside, the whole garden gets watered. When the sun shines, roses and weeds alike reap the benefit. What's growing in the garden has no choice but to take the weather as it comes. The daisies can't scamper for cover, and you won't find the veggies huddling in the shade (unless you planted them there!)

Planted as we are in God's garden; however, we can reject God's good gifts and spurn His desire to love us. Although He wants us to thrive under the sweet and nourishing showers of His promises, we can choose to remain in an arid and barren spiritual desert. While His will is for us to bask in the warm light of His never-ending presence, we might prefer to linger in the chilly shadows of doubt or unbelief.

The Holy Spirit waits at the door of your heart with the spiritual weather you need most at this time and season of your life—maybe gentle showers of consolation or dynamic winds of change. Perhaps He feels you need a period of quiet rest or extraordinary growth, sprouting seeds or abundant fruitfulness. Whatever He sends, it's going to be a perfect day for you!

A small seed placed in the furrow to grow shrank...Shriveling hurt until the sun drew forth from the ache a leaf.

CLAIRE PEDRETTI

Shout Out

Let me thrive today, Lord!

What Do You Know?

*I ask ... the God of glory—to make you intelligent
and discerning in knowing him personally.*
EPHESIANS 1:17 THE MESSAGE

We're people interested in people! When an athlete takes home the trophy, fans might want to know where she was born, where she trained, and what motivated her to pursue her sport. A historical figure piques our interest, and we read that person's biography so we can find out more about his or her work and life.

In the Bible, you can find out quite a bit about God. It will tell you about the things He has said and done, His love for the world and His plan of salvation, and how He wants His people to live their lives. While these are important truths for you to know about God, even more important is for you to know Him! He desires a personal and intimate relationship with you, one that goes beyond your head-knowledge and all the way to your heart-knowledge.

From simply acquainting yourself with facts about Him, hear Him invite you to a fuller, richer, and more rewarding understanding of His presence in your everyday life. As you read, reflect, and pray, let God transform information to awareness, knowing about Him to knowing Him.

We know God easily,
if we do not constrain ourselves
to define him.

JOSEPH JOUBERT

Shout Out

I want to know more—I want to know You!

My Problem, His Answer

Commit thy works unto the Lord,
and thy thoughts shall be established

PROVERBS 16:3 KJV

If you enjoy solving crossword puzzles, you've probably experienced something like this: You've read the clue, you have three letters of the answer filled in, but you just can't come up with a word that fits. So you put down the puzzle and don't give it another thought. Then, hours later, you glance back at the puzzle and voilà! The answer is obvious, and you wonder why you hadn't thought of it earlier.

Personal problems, even serious ones, can be like that, too. We know full well what the issue is, but we don't have an immediate solution. Rather than temporarily letting it go, however, we keep on it. It's all we can think about during the day, and it keeps us tossing and turning at night. Still, we're no closer to an answer. Now that anxiety has amplified the issue, we might even conclude that there is no answer.

God asks you to take your problems to Him and leave them there for a practical purpose. Not only are you showing your trust in His wisdom, you're freeing your mind. And that's when you're most likely to discover the answer in plain sight!

*We cannot always understand
the ways of Almighty God....
But we accept with faith
his holy will.*

ROSE FITZGERALD KENNEDY

Shout Out
No problem—God has the answer!

On Steady Ground

*Plant your roots in Christ and let him
be the foundation for your life.
Be strong in your faith.*
COLOSSIANS 2:7 CEV

A troubled relationship. A failed venture. Job loss. Deflating criticism. These can shake our self-confidence to the core. But how about people who explain away, or completely discount, biblical events? What about those who look down on the community of faith, or friends who seem to get along just fine without God? For our spiritual confidence, these are nothing short of earthquakes!

If you're among people, you can't avoid skeptics and scoffers, cynics and unbelievers. While they may have made up their minds long ago, don't let them make up yours, too. Reflect on the time-honored truths of Scripture, and listen as God's Word speaks to you. Recall the still small voice that has brought comfort to your heart in times of need. Remember the promises of God and ask yourself if you want to rely on His Word or on the word of others.

When you feel your spiritual confidence start to wobble, set the feet of your beliefs on solid ground. Rely on the foundation of faith the Holy Spirit is building in your heart and soul. The more firmly you stand on it, the stronger it gets!

*Doubt is looking for the light;
unbelief is content
with darkness.*

JOHN DRUMMOND

Shout Out

*I'm standing strong on my
foundation of faith!*

Clean Out the Clutter

Leave behind your foolishness and begin to live;
learn how to be wise.

PROVERBS 9:6 TLB

If you have ever gone through stacks of boxes that have been stored in the attic for years, you might have come across an old moldy jigsaw puzzle with half the pieces missing. "Why in the world are we keeping this?" you ask. It's of no use to anyone!

The regrets you store in your heart are like that old moldy jigsaw puzzle. You regret wrong decisions and ill-advised choices. The opportunities you missed and the risks you didn't take. The words you said and those you neglected to say. Yet the pieces missing from each regret are a full recollection of your perspective, your needs and fears, and your circumstances at the time. From every experience in the past, you learned something about the world and about yourself that has made you a wiser person today.

So why in the world are you keeping that old moldy regret? It's no use to anyone, least of all to you! All it's doing is taking up room in your heart that the Holy Spirit longs to fill with compassion, forgiveness, and gratitude. That would be a much better use of the space.

*The past cannot be changed;
the future is still in your power.*

HUGH LAWSON WHITE

Finding Our Root

*Therefore encourage one another and build each
other up as you are already doing.*
1 THESSALONIANS 5:11 HCSB

Imagine an iconic autumn scene: a cluster of stately aspen trees, their vibrant yellow leaves shimmering against a clear blue sky. While you're picturing individual trees, underground it's a different story. The entire cluster of aspens shares the same root system.

Although each of us possesses an individual identity, underneath it all we share the same life-giving root, our Creator-God. His Spirit works in all who are willing to let Him, enabling good spiritual health not only for us personally, but for our entire "cluster"—family, community, nation, world. A soul trying to cut itself off from its root weakens the cluster, while a soul growing stronger in faith and love fortifies and beautifies the cluster. The spiritual condition of each of us matters to all of us.

God did not create you to be a spiritual lone tree, but one firmly connected to Him and actively interconnected with others. Let your words and actions, the "leaves" of good spiritual health, influence others. Support and encourage them as they flourish with you, connected with the living and life-giving root of all, our Creator-God.

If seed in the black earth can turn into such beautiful roses, what might not the heart of man become in its long journey toward the stars?

G. K. CHESTERTON

Shout Out

My good spiritual health blesses everyone around me!

More Than a Market

The Lord will send His faithful love by day;
His song will be with me in the night— a prayer
to the God of my life.

PSALM 42:8 HCSB

When you need groceries, you might make a list and take a trip to your local supermarket. Otherwise, (unless you work there!) you probably won't go back until your cupboards start to look bare again.

God invites you to bring your list of needs, wants, and requests to Him in prayer, and He promises to listen and respond according to His wisdom. But prayer is so much more than a spiritual supermarket, not visited again until your heart's cupboard feels bare and you have another long list in your hands. Prayer is also an opportunity to express to God your feelings for Him and your gratitude for all He does for you. It's a time to lay your burdens at His feet and receive the comfort of His forgiveness and assurance of His love. Prayer offers you a unique occasion to simply let your heart sing for the happiness of His presence and the joy of belonging to Him.

Go to God in prayer every day, even several times a day. And occasionally go without your list. Call on Him without *needing* anything, except the pleasure of telling your God how glad you are to know Him!

He thought that prayer
was talking.
But he became more
and more quiet
until in the end he realized
that prayer is listening.

SOREN KIERKEGAARD

Shout Out
Thank You, God, for everything!

Time Table

There's an opportune time to do things, a right time for everything on the earth.
ECCLESIASTES 3:1 THE MESSAGE

We're creatures of habit. We get used to eating breakfast, lunch, and dinner at set hours. We catch the TV shows we always watch, spend our free time in certain ways, go to bed and get up as usual. But often as we grow and mature spiritually, we realize we want adjust our schedules to accommodate more time with God.

If you've outgrown the God-time you've allotted for yourself, examine your daily routine. Some to-do's probably aren't changeable, like when you leave for work or drop the kids off at school. Other things, however, are personal choices, and these are usually quite flexible. Some are habits that you're so used to doing that they seem set in stone! They aren't. For example, the time you spend checking your emails and social media accounts. Could you shorten it? How about the time you spend in front of the TV. Maybe you aren't as interested in those shows as you used to be.

Go through your day hour by hour and look for a couple of time-saving options. You're likely to discover you have more time for God than you expected—and perhaps for a few other worthwhile things, too!

The small moment is the carrier of God's most endearing gift. It must not be permitted to slip away unsavored or unappreciated.

GERHARD E. FROST

Shout Out

I'll make time for God-time!

It's Very Personal

He has granted to us His precious and magnificent promises, so that by them you may become partakers of the divine nature.

2 PETER 1:4 NASB

You relate to a friend the offensive remark you heard from someone. "Ignore it," she tells you. "Don't take it personally." That's certainly wise advice for any careless or ill-considered comment you might come across!

God's Word, however, is something you do want to take personally. Very personally. Not one of His promises was made without His clear intention, or outside His will and power to carry it through. Even more, His scriptural promises apply to you. When He promises that He will hear your prayers, He means exactly what He says. When He promises to forgive you when you come to Him with a repentant heart, He won't go back on His pledge, no matter what it is that you've done. When He promises to be there for you wherever you may be, you can go to the bank with it.

Joy. Peace. Rest. Strength. Help. Comfort. When it's one of God's promises, do take it personally. Expect it to happen. Apply it to your thoughts, words, and actions. Live it in your day-to-day life. God's promises are meant for you personally.

God is the God of promises.
He keeps his word, even when
that seems impossible.

COLIN URQUHART

Shout Out

If You promise it, Lord, I believe it!

No Small Print

All need to be made right with God by his grace,
which is a free gift.

ROMANS 3:24 NCV

God's grace is free. Hard to believe, isn't it? We expect to see an asterisk that takes us down to the bottom of the page for a small-print list of exclusions. We wonder if perhaps this is one of those too-good-to-be-true come-ons that fill our mailboxes these days. We look for the strings attached, the terms and conditions, the honest-to-God truth.

Because God is complete holiness, what He says is nothing but the truth. That's why you can take what He says at full face value. His grace is free to you today! No trial period. No serving an internship, proving yourself, jumping through hoops. It's not a reward for good behavior, it's grace, poured on you by God by His power and His decision. Long before you could crawl out of your crib, His grace was yours. Simply yours. So why try to make it complicated now?

Bask in this great truth for a few minutes. Remove from your thoughts anything you imagine might earn you even a drop of grace, and focus your heart on God. He is the grace-giver. And it's free—honest to God!

*Grace is given not because we have done good works,
but in order that we may be able to do them.*

SAINT AUGUSTINE

Shout Out

Thank You! Thank You! Thank You!

The Good Life

He offered himself as a sacrifice to free us from
a dark, rebellious life into this good, pure life.
TITUS 2:14 THE MESSAGE

What's your idea of the "good life"? Endless wealth, ease, and enjoyment is a popular answer, but if you're like most people, it isn't a realistic expectation. How about a life dedicated to giving every bit of your time, resources, and abilities to charity? Right now, though, you're using most all of those gifts to meet your personal responsibilities.

So let's look at the "good life," which is neither an improbable reality nor a bid for sainthood. Your good life begins with a true appreciation of and sincere gratitude for God's abundant grace and His never-ending love. That's the firm and reliable basis for the good life that His Spirit desires to provide for you. Next comes your desire to follow Him. Your openness to His counsel and obedience to His teachings turn your everyday life into the good life. By making God-pleasing decisions, you avoid many personal struggles and pitfalls. By relying on His strength instead of your own, you have what it takes to withstand life's difficulties and hardships.

The good life begins with God, and God works from the inside out. He's ready to start building immediately!

*The key to living the good life
is love—and true unselfish love
comes only from God.*

ANGELA DRAKE

Shout Out
I'm living the good life!

Back to Basics

You must, of course, continue faithful on a firm and sure foundation.

COLOSSIANS 1:23 GNT

The prima ballerina, ethereal in her long romantic tutu, takes her bows after a spectacular performance. The applause goes on and on, and bouquets come one after the other. Yet after the curtain goes down on a memorable evening, the next morning she's back in the studio, dressed in an ordinary leotard and tights, and going through the elements of her craft—the basic steps. She knows that her strength and mastery rest not on magical performances, but on everyday application and constant practice.

Our spiritual knowledge begins with an introduction to who God is, His feelings toward us, and His plan for our salvation. Basic stuff! But without grasping these truths, we're likely to stumble when we start reflecting on some of the challenging truths that God presents to us for our continued growth, strength, and maturity. If we're too eager to experience awesome moments with God, we're like a beginning dancer who enrolls in an advanced class. Disappointment and frustration are certain!

There's something else, too. No matter how long you have been a God-follower, don't forget the basics. God is love. He yearns for you to know Him, and He wants you for eternity.

When you walk with God,
you get where he is going.

AUTHOR UNKNOWN

Shout Out

Lord, may I have this dance?

River of Life

He shewed me a pure river of water of life,
clear as crystal, proceeding out of the throne of
God and of the Lamb.

REVELATION 22:1 KJV

A river runs through it! Today's river city usually has the waterway to thank for its location. The river provided early settlers with food, water, and transportation. As the town grew, the river offered a source of energy for industry and brought jobs to the community. Today the river might also host recreational swimming, canoe regattas, and kayak races. Its scenic banks have attracted art galleries and restaurants, pricey condos and picnic grounds. The river is the life of the city!

Your relationship with God is like a river running through your heart and soul. Its flowing waters bring you spiritual blessings, and its life-giving waters slake your thirst and feed your spirit. Its mighty waters provide you with power to live according to His will, and its restoring waters bring you rest, refreshment, and joy. Because the river of God runs through you, your heart is a place of growth, contentment, and prosperity. Through your words and actions, you attract others and influence them for the better.

The next time you cross a bridge, look down at the river, a source of life. Reflect on the source of life that flows through you.

God is above, presiding;
beneath, sustaining;
within, filling.

HILDEBERT OF LAVARDIN

Shout Out

I'm going with the flow—God's flow!

SECTION 3

Those who plant in tears will harvest with shouts of joy.

PSALM 126:5 NLT

Welcome Home

You were like sheep going astray,
but have now returned to the Shepherd
and Overseer of your souls.

1 PETER 2:25 NKJV

If you have a navigation system in your car, you might have had this experience. You took a wrong turn, and then another one, and now you're completely lost. What a relief to pull over, reach for the device, and press "Go Home." Within minutes, you're back on a familiar road and headed for home!

In life, everyone makes a wrong turn now and then. A road looks attractive, so we take it. We think we'll be smart and try a shortcut. Or we have to admit it—we just aren't paying attention. Now we're in unfamiliar territory and definitely not where we intended to be. Say, hanging around people who want us to do things their way, not God's way. Falling into unhealthy habits, and not feeling good about ourselves. Where is the "Go Home" button?

It's right where you are, wherever you are. There's no place God isn't, so never doubt His presence. Lift your thoughts to Him in prayer, turn your attention to His counsel and guidelines, and let Him navigate you back to your heart's home with Him.

*Right actions for the future
are the best apologies
for wrong ones in the past.*

TYRON EDWARDS

Shout Out

Turn my heart and mind to You, Lord!

The Best of Creation

In the beginning God created the heavens and the earth.

GENESIS 1:1 NASB

When God called the universe into being, our world was flawless. Imagine unspoiled earth and sky, land and seas, flowers and fields, mountains and valleys. What a breathtaking sight the world must have been, because God created everything absolutely perfect, inside and out.

In our lives, we create things. We might establish a home for ourselves and our loved ones. Many among us build products or provide services to buyers, clients, and customers. Others form or join associations created to help and assist those in need. But are our creations perfect? Far from it, and we know that! But with God's original creation as our high standard, we hold ourselves to high standards in whatever we do. God didn't scrimp or cheat or cut corners when He made the world for us, and that's why what we create—goods or services, physical things or intangible concepts—deserves nothing short of our best effort.

Name the most awe-inspiring nature scene you can think of. Look to a clear blue sky or deep red rose. Let it remind you of the joy, pleasure, and privilege of your ability to create!

God made us in his image and likeness.
Therefore we are creators

DOROTHY MAY DAY

Shout Out
I will do my best in whatever I do!

Holding Hands

Lead me to do your will; make your way plain
for me to follow.
PSALM 5:8 GNT

Picture a toddler scampering happily along the sidewalk. Relishing all the delights around her, she's oblivious to the pitted pavement, preoccupied pedestrians, and four lanes of rush-hour traffic only a few feet away. Within seconds, her mother reaches down, grabs her hand, and holds it firmly until they reach the playground at the end of the street.

Though we're grown-ups now, there's a little of that toddler in us. We're engrossed in our work, enthralled by entertainment, and beguiled by the attractions our world has to offer. Skipping happily along, we let our God-time shrink and our spiritual nourishment languish. Danger ahead! That's when our heavenly Father reaches down, grabs our hands, and pulls us back closer to Him. Like the toddler, we might protest. We were having a lot of fun! And yes, we can yank our hand out of His and continue on our merry way. Hey, we're grown-ups, aren't we?

Often a resonating word of Scripture, the cautionary tale of a friend, or a minor stumble is God's way of reaching down and taking you by the hand. Rest it in His, and let Him lead you to the safety of His way.

*Christ leads me through
no darker rooms than
he went through before.*

RICHARD BAXTER

Shout Out

Take me by the hand, Lord!

A Joyful Heart

Your mercies, God, run into the billions;
following your guidelines, revive me.
PSALM 119:155 THE MESSAGE

When you think about what it means to be a Christian, what comes to mind? For many, the response is some variation of "rules," "self-denial," and "no fun." Sadly, they are missing one of those "rules" they might like to hear: Set your heart on joy. Live it. And yes, have fun!

A relationship with God through Jesus brings joy—soul- and heart-deep joy. His Spirit empowers you to embrace joy, to make it real in your life by gladly accepting His authority over you and willingly following Him. As joy grows, so does your ability to accept that His guidelines are always meant to bless you, even when you can't imagine how. With reliance on His wisdom over yours, you're free to happily relax and truly delight in your day. You'll discover the joy of simple pleasures, the joy of God-sent gladness, and the joy of being you.

God made known His guidelines not to withhold from you, but to give to you; not to see you frown, but to see you smile; not to make life hard, but to make life nothing less than joyful. Will you let Him?

Joy is the gigantic secret
of the Christian.

G.K. CHESTERTON

Shout Out

I choose joy!

Because of Jesus

Jesus is not ashamed to call us his brothers.

HEBREWS 2:11 TLB

From here, God looks pretty intimidating. Way up there, on a throne high in the heavens, sits the all-powerful, all-seeing, all-knowing presence who has ultimate say-so over all things human. What's more, He is holy, and He demands pure holiness in His presence. Given those truths, it's not surprising that we're acutely aware of our shortcomings. How could He love us? It doesn't make sense! Why would a perfect God pour love on imperfect us?

God's Son, Jesus, was born among us not to explain why God loves us (as if we'd get it!), but to show what God's love is. Through His miracles, Jesus demonstrated that God's love is more than spiritual, extending to our everyday needs, such as physical health and well-being. Through His compassion, He revealed that God's love leads Him to forgive our sins and strengthen our faith. Through His death and resurrection, He demonstrated God's power over the worst evil, death. Will His love raise us up to His holiness? Yes!

Jesus bridges the distance between you and your heavenly Father. Because of Jesus, it's not what you see, but what God sees—a purely holy child, dearly loved, and welcome in His presence.

Jesus bridges the gap between God's perfect holiness and the deeply flawed soul of man.

ANNA RESTON

Shout Out

I am not afraid because I am His!

Plans and Counter-Plans

*I've got my eye on the goal, where God
is beckoning us onward—to Jesus.*

PHILIPPIAN 3:24 THE MESSAGE

Some people establish a goal and then pursue it with all they've got. Others decide they'll see what comes along, floating from one thing to the next, as a ship adrift in a bobbing sea. The first way of life fixes your eyes so solidly on one objective that you're blind to promising openings and sensational opportunities along the way. You missed them because you never saw them! The second offers no real satisfaction. Going with the flow, you never stay any-place long enough to enjoy its true riches.

Which is the best way? A balance between the two, of course. Have short- and long-term goals, because they give your life meaning and purpose, and they give you something to work toward. At the same time, remain flexible so you won't fear to grab hold of opportunities God may send your way—opportunities far surpassing anything you could have foreseen. What a loss to you and those who would have benefited from your presence, if you shy away because His opportunity doesn't match your plans!

So sure, set goals. They keep you headed in the right direction. But when God sends opportunities, arise and take them!

*The great opportunity
is where you are.*

JOHN BURROUGHS

Shout Out

God's plans are my plans!

A Heart of Thanks

I will give You thanks with all my heart;
I will sing Your praise before the heavenly beings.
PSALM 100:1 HCSB

Rather than spend her money on a small luxury for herself, she picks out a gift she thinks her granddaughter will love. Instead of going away for the weekend, he uses the money to buy his niece the prom dress that her parents can't afford. Months after sending the gifts, however, no thank-you notes have arrived. No phone calls; no texts. Though both girls were ecstatic to get the gifts, each forgot something more important than the gifts—they overlooked the giver.

Whether we are faithful or forgetful when it comes to writing thank-you notes, we're all-too-often neglectful when it comes to thanking God—the giver of all good things. He showers us with gifts all year long. Do we take them for granted? He sends us the particular blessing we have longed for and prayed for, and now we're so happy! Are we so enamored with the gift that we lose sight of the one from whom it came?

Look around you and see God's good gifts spreading out in every direction. Recall a recent special request that He has graciously granted. Perhaps a heartfelt thank-You prayer is in order right now.

*Were there no God,
we would be in this glorious
world with grateful hearts
and no one to thank.*

CHRISTINA ROSSETTI

Shout Out

I will live with a thankful heart!

An Empty Place

*His presence within us is God's guarantee
that he really will give us all that he promised.*

EPHESIANS 1:14 TLB

Maybe it's the loss of a loved one, a dear friend, or a beloved pet. Loss leaves a space in the heart that nothing else can fill. Yes, time will dim the pain somewhat, but your thoughts and memories will bring you back to the special life you once knew so deeply, so intimately.

Not far beyond the beginning of time, loss came into the world. It happened when human pride pushed God away and chose none other than itself as the object of affection. Our perfect relationship with God lost, an empty place remains in the human heart to this day. Over the millennia, people have tried to fill it with possessions and wealth, to satisfy its longing with fame and accomplishment, entertainment and self-indulgence. But nothing worked because the empty place belongs to God. It's where He longs to dwell. It's what He yearns to fill with His gifts, His joy, His presence.

When the empty space in your heart is God's, invite Him in. His presence comforts, soothes, and eases you in every loss. Let the one who created your heart live in your heart always.

*God and man
exist for each other
and neither is satisfied
without the other.*

A. W. TOZER

Shout Out

Fill my heart, Lord, with You!

The Difference is God

Good people, rejoice and be happy in the Lord.
Sing all you whose hearts are right.

PSALM 32:11 NCV

As a God-follower, you probably speak and act pretty much like anyone else of high standards and goodwill. You step up, pitch in, and help out. You're cheerful, always ready with a smile for the people you meet. You're faithful to your family and friends. You work hard, and you're fair and honest with everyone. But underneath appearances, there's a big difference because you love God, and that's what motivates you day by day.

God's Spirit has planted within you a motivator that far surpasses a desire to "be a good person." You possess the Spirit-given ability and willingness to think, speak, and act for His glory and the benefit of others. While a self-empowered wish to be known as "good" may melt in the heat of temptation or cool in the winds of convenience, Spirit-powered goodness is not so easily overcome. You have His strength to shield you, and His wisdom and guidance to draw on.

On the surface, you might not seem much different from many others around you. But underneath it all, it's another story. You're very different, and your connection to Christ makes it that way!

Let each man think of himself
as an act of God,
his mind a thought of God,
his life a breath of God.

PHILIP JAMES BAILEY

Shout Out

I make a difference because I am different!

A Lesson in Give and Take

Happy is the person who finds wisdom,
the one who gets understanding.

PROVERBS 3:13 NCV

Classroom teachers often say that they learn as much from students as students learn from them—and maybe more! As their students gain practical knowledge, teachers increase in heart knowledge. There's no better way to acquire empathy, compassion, and understanding than by engaging in lively interaction with people of all ages and backgrounds.

If you are just starting out on God's path, mature God-followers are a valuable resource for you to draw on. They have scriptural knowledge to teach you and real-world experience to share. But you're not simply a spiritual sponge, able only to soak up what you see and hear! You, too, have much to give. Your honest and forthright questions compel those who teach to examine their faith and delve deeply for answers. Your requests for guidance allow them the privilege of exercising their God-given ability to extend comfort and care. Your eagerness to learn animates their readiness to teach.

On the spiritual path, all of us are learners, because we don't outgrow our need to search the heights and depths of God's ways with us. And all of us are teachers as we travel ahead, beside, and behind one another in faith and love.

We cannot hold a torch
to light another's path
without brightening our own.

BEN SWEETLAND

Shout Out
I will generously give as I gratefully take!

Peace That Lasts

The Lord gives his people strength.
The Lord blesses them with peace.

PSALM 29:11 NLT

There's not much peace happening in the world today—actually, there never has been. Our beautiful but broken world is host to a long history of unrest, conflicts, disasters, and tragedies on a local, national, and global scale. So when Jesus spoke to His disciples about peace, the word must have sounded as unrealistic to them as it does to us!

Yet peace is what God extends to you. It's real, it's powerful, and it's yours to use and enjoy, savor and share today. Your Spirit-infused peace enables you to hear today's newscast without despairing, remembering that the world is still God's world, and He is in control. The peace you hold in your heart raises your eyes above personal fears, failures, illnesses, worries, and disappointments to see your God, the one who is still guarding you, still guiding you, and still loving you.

When God, through Jesus, pronounces peace on you, you have peace—a real-world, resilient, never-yielding, and up-to-the-minute peace. Whether it's what's going on across the globe or in your own backyard that threatens to disturb your peace, stand on His. It will hold forever.

Finding God,
You have no need to seek peace,
for he himself is your peace.

FRANCES J. ROBERTS

Shout Out

God's peace is stronger than my fears!

A Life of Contrasts

*You are my hiding place; you protect me
from trouble. You surround me
with songs of victory.*

PSALM 32:7 NLT

To create her quilt, she carefully moves different colors of fabric together and then stands back. Yes, the light shades make the dark shades pop. The middle tones allow the eye to rest until captured again by the excitement of black against white, red against yellow, pale orange against vivid purple. It's the stark contrasts that will give the quilt its unique look, beauty, and meaning.

Each life, too, is one of contrasts. A blissfully happy time—maybe years!—might rest side by side with dark, difficult days. A time of loss, say the passing of a beloved elder, may be followed by one of gain—the birth of a new grandchild. A time of uncertainty morphs into a period of steady growth. A muted interval of struggle moves into a bright, exciting phase of achievement and celebration. A stretch of spiritual effort is followed by a space of God-sent rest and understanding.

Would heights of gladness seem as exceptional if you had never known life's lows? Would an overwhelming sense of God's presence be as comforting if you had never experienced His apparent distance? Contrast is part of God's plan—His plan for your unique, beautiful, and meaningful life.

Satan whispers,
"All is lost."
God says,
"Much can be gained."

FRANCES J. ROBERTS

Shout Out

Highs and lows? They go together!

Made by Hand

He created them male and female,
and He blessed them.
GENESIS 5:2 NASB

We enjoy receiving gifts that have been thoughtfully chosen and graciously given. But how about gifts that are thoughtfully chosen, graciously given, and lovingly made by hand? Those gifts often mean the most, because we know that the giver spent more than money. They spent their time, talents, and effort to create a one-of-a-kind gift just for us.

Have you ever seen yourself as God's one-of-a-kind gift? His unique handiwork? His blessing to those around you? Wherever you go, you're bringing your personal perspective, individual abilities, and distinctive presence—and not by chance, because God is not one to waste the work of His hands. Perhaps your caring helps a loved one cope or a friend survive a tough time. Maybe your understanding calms a troubled heart, or your smile lifts a sagging mood. Then again, it could be a past experience of yours that gives you the knowledge allowing you to help where no one else can!

You have been lovingly made by God's hand. He has thoughtfully chosen you, and He has graciously given you your life for a purpose. Wherever you go today, know that no one but one-of-a-kind you will do!

God passes through
the thicket of the world,
and wherever his glance falls,
he turns all things to beauty.

PHILIP JAMES BAILEY

Shout Out

I am thoughtfully and skillfully made!

Time of Your Life

Rest in the Lord and wait patiently for Him.
PSALM 37:7 NASB

If you want time to slow down, try watching the clock for fifteen minutes! With each passing second, the gap between them seems to stretch longer and longer, while you're getting more and more impatient. Five minutes later, you're ready to take the clock and throw it against the wall!

As you wait for God to unfold His plans for you, are you watching the clock? Say nothing is happening that you believe shows His movement within you, much less what you would like to see take place around you. You get antsy! This is just taking to long! You think through your day-to-day experience and find no spiritual progress or demonstrable sign of His presence. So you watch the clock a few minutes more, and then you give up. Does God have anything to do with your life at all?

It's not easy to see sometimes, but God has everything to do with your life, your purpose, and your plans. Instead of "watching the clock," spend your time reflecting on His Word and appreciating what He has for you right now. Be patient. His time is always the right time.

Time is a precious gift of God;
so precious that he only gives it
to us moment by moment.

AMELIA EDITH BARR

Shout Out
I can wait on God!

It Just Keeps On Coming!

I will sing of your steadfast love,
O Lord, forever.

PSALM 89:1 NRSV

If you spend time at the beach, you know that the ocean waves just keep coming and coming and coming! The ebb and flow, swoosh and sweep, silence and swell are the same now as they have been for millennia, despite upheavals, pollution, and the passage of time.

God's love is like those persistent ocean waves—it keeps coming day after day, year after year. What's going on outside of you—the chaos, confusion, and commotion—and what's going on inside you—the anxieties, worries, and fears—don't change the nature or intensity of God's love. Like waves, sin, guilt, shame, and regret crash onto the shore of your life, but God's love just keeps on coming as well. Waves of despair, loneliness, hopelessness? God's love is always there to meet them.

When you look at the ocean waves sweeping over the sandy shoreline, let what you see remind you of the love that just keeps coming despite everything. Think of the power, depth, and breadth of God's love. It's mightier, deeper, and wider than any body of water imaginable! And it's more plentiful, too. Wherever you are, immerse yourself in His unstoppable love!

God's love is measureless.
It is more;
it is boundless.

A.W. TOZER

Shout Out

God will never run out of love for me!

Where Are You?

With you is the fountain of life;
in your light we see light.
PSALM 36:9 NRSV

As a housewarming gift, a couple happily received a potted plant from a friend. Although the tag said to place the plant in full sunlight, the happy homeowners put it where they thought it looked best—the corner of a large, dim room. There's no denying that the plant provided a welcome spot of life and greenery to the area, but after a few months, leaves drooped and the plant languished.

Unlike the hapless plant, you can choose where you place yourself. Although God says you need the sunlight of His wisdom and guidance every day, you are free to put yourself in the shadows of self-direction and self-empowerment. You can go where others praise you for being one of their own, for looking the other way, for deciding what's practical in this day and age. But how about what God said you really need? What about sunlight?

Ask God to move you into His light—that is, the light of His Son, Jesus. Thrive where the words of His care, comfort, compassion, and love stream down on you every day, day after day. Let Him show you your place in the Son. That's where you belong!

*God is a light
that is never darkened;
an unwearied life
that cannot die;
a fountain always flowing;
a garden of life.*

FRANCIS QUARLES

Shout Out

Warm me in the light of Your Sonshine!

What Does God Want?

Our Lord Jesus Christ has made us friends of God.
ROMANS 5:11 NLT

"What do you want?" We might be asking the question out of genuine concern, or a desire to please, or even a feeling of exasperation. The tone of voice says it all when we're talking to one another, as well as when we're talking with God.

Prompted by anxiety over our relationship with God, we urge Him to tell us clearly what we can do to win His favor. Or hoping to impress Him, we perform a self-concocted sacrificial feat. Or because we don't know how many good deeds are sufficient for Him, we scream in frustration, "God, what do you want?" His answer? "To live within you." Yes, that's all. When we allow His Spirit to actively nourish, direct, and develop our lives, everything else falls into place. He loved us first, so we have no need to worry about our worthiness. He has a joyful and purposeful plan for our lives, so we don't have to think up something extraordinary to do, or tally up all the good deeds we've done hoping to impress Him.

What does God want? Simply to have a living relationship with you and bless you with His presence and love.

God seeks comrades
and claims love;
the devil seeks slaves
and claims obedience.

SIR RABINDRANATH TAGORE

Shout Out

I want You to live in me!

Walk Fearlessly

I am trusting you, O Lord, saying,
"You are my God!"

PSALM 31:14 NLT

It's unlikely you remember, but it happened, didn't it? As a very young child, you learned to walk by holding onto the edge of a low table and toddling along, step by careful step. Then one day, you let go. Ta-da! No more table to hold you back. You were free to go!

Adulthood can find us clinging to tables, too. Even though they're invisible, they're real. We may have become so accustomed to depending on others to make our decisions that we're terrified to step out on our own. We may have felt afraid for so long that we can't imagine living without fear. We never venture away from it, because who knows what might happen? We may be hanging onto an old negative self-image from our teen years that we just can't shake, even though it hardly describes the women we are today.

What "table" props you up? Can you let go of it? Yes! With God, stand confidently, because you trust in Him. Walk fearlessly, because you know He's there to pick you up if you should stumble. Run freely and joyfully, because that's exactly what you can do!

I would rather walk with God
in the dark
than walk alone
in the light.

MARY GARDINER BRAINARD

Shout Out

I can stand, walk, and run
—no props needed!

A Penny for Your Thoughts

You know when I sit down and when I stand up;
You understand my thoughts from far away.

PSALM 139:2 HCSB

As soon as the words left her mouth, she wanted to pull them back again. True, they were exactly what was going through her mind, but she never intended to say it out loud, much less to her best friend. Now her hastily cobbled together apology feels phony. Does it sound phony, too? Although her friend graciously overlooks the slight, a shadow falls across their relationship.

Most all of us can relate to the story. An ugly word slips, an inappropriate remark sneaks out, a mean-spirited thought is voiced. When unkindly words occupy the heart, we shouldn't be surprised when—not if—they tumble out of our mouths. That's why God's Spirit works from inside us, starting with the heart. The love He creates there draws us away from harsh to gentle thoughts, from judgmental to compassionate thoughts. Like a sweet fragrance, this love infuses not just what we're thinking, but what we're saying, too.

What are you thinking? When the Spirit of God is the source of your thoughts, you're free to say what you think, no apologies needed!

Little keys can open big locks.
Simple words can express
great thoughts.

WILLIAM ARTHUR WARD

Shout Out

My words and thoughts go together!

Everyone Means You

Let him that is athirst come. And whosoever will,
let him take the water of life freely.
REVELATION 22:17 KJV

"Everyone's welcome to come to my house," the couple says to their friends seated around the restaurant table. They happily smile and nod and promise to be there. Of course, they don't really mean everyone—not, say, the people seated around a table on the other side of the room. Not everyone who lives in the same town or city or state. Not the whole world, for pity's sake! Their "everyone" is clearly and obviously limited.

God's "everyone" truly is unlimited. When He invites everyone to come to Him, He means everyone in the world! The call that goes out to those who have wandered from His path is the same call He extends to His longtime followers. He offers comfort, forgiveness, compassion, and peace of mind and heart to all people, even to those who willfully and deliberately exclude Him from their lives. He begs to restore, renew, and revitalize the souls of every person who calls Him a friend and every person who calls Him an enemy.

God's "everyone" has no limits. His love is open to all, and there's love enough for all. That's why when He says "everyone," He means you!

*God loves each of us
as if there were only
one of us.*

SAINT AUGUSTINE

Shout Out

Here I am, Lord!

Comfort Food

*Blessed be the God ... who comforts us ...
that we may be able to comfort those
who are in any trouble.*

2 CORINTHIANS 1:3-4 NKJV

Ahhh, comfort food! There's nothing like it to warm us on a cold, snowy night—evoking memories of Mom's bright, busy kitchen and whetting the appetite like nothing else does. And if you know how to make satisfying, savory meals for others, it's most likely that someone once made them for you. You've got the recipe!

The comfort we're able to bring to others isn't something we need to "cook up" for ourselves. It's the comfort we receive from God when we mourn our losses, setbacks, and disappointments. As His Spirit feeds us with trust in His wisdom, faith in His strength, and hope for our future, we are comforted. Now we have the recipe. Far from sweet-sounding platitudes, we can offer nutritious morsels of God's care and consolation. We can tell about His strength that never fails, His presence that never changes, and His power to work all things for our ultimate good. We can give soul-warming comfort, because that's what He has given us.

If you mourn, go to Him for comfort. If you know someone who could use comforting, invite them for a feast. God's kitchen is always open.

God does not comfort us
to make us comfortable
but to make us comforters.

JOHN HENRY JOWETT

Shout Out

I will comfort others just as God comforts me!

A Song to Sing

I will sing to the Lord as long as I live;
I will sing praise to my God
while I have my being.

PSALM 104:33 NKJV

Have you ever awakened to the sound of a solitary bird singing in the breaking dawn? Have you lingered at the window, letting the cheery chirps from a single warbler charm you into a smile? The little songsters sing wherever they happen to be, and perhaps for no other reason than that they have a song to sing!

You don't need to have a special reason to talk to God. There's no need to plan your words or prepare a formal speech or recite a time-honored prayer before God will bend His ear to you. Why wait until you're in a bind to immerse yourself in the joy of His presence? God is everywhere! Where you live and work, exercise and play. He's open to your spontaneous prayers and extemporaneous bursts of thanksgiving wherever the thought pops into your mind. When you want to sing, He's delighted to hear the sound of your voice!

Sometimes the most beautiful song is the one sung from an ordinary branch, on an ordinary tree, in an ordinary place, on an ordinary day, just for the pleasure of singing.

Music is God's best gift to man,
the only art of heaven
given to earth,
the only art of earth
we take to heaven.

LETITIA E. LANDON

Shout Out

Wherever I am, my heart will sing!

Confidence and Humility

If you are wise and understand God's ways,
prove it by living an honorable life.
JAMES 3:13 NLT

When you picture a humble person, what do you see? A gray-robed figure with bowed head silently and unobtrusively tiptoeing along a shadowed corridor? Or do you see someone so scrupulous about putting others first that she never shares her ideas or interests, much less her successes? Though extreme examples, many of us who desire to be humble can see ourselves reflected in them.

Godly, genuine humility is not the opposite of, but a companion to, godly and genuine self-confidence. While self-confidence empowers you to speak up as someone worthy of being heard, humility teaches you that yours is not the only voice in the room. Your self-confidence enables you to share your trials and triumphs with others, and humility turns your attention to the trials and triumphs of others, too. It's self-confidence that banishes social fears and anxieties, and it's humility that places you among equals, all beloved children of God.

As a confident person, stand up straight and make eye contact with the world! And as a humble person, walk gently, smile, and open your hands and heart to everyone around you.

*I am as my creator made me,
and since he is satisfied,
so am I.*

MINNIE SMITH

Shout Out

Humbly, I will look the world in the eye!

Your Faith Is Showing!

I planted the seed in your hearts
...but it was God who made it grow.
1 CORINTHIANS 3:6 NLT

Peel an orange and drop a seed into the ground. Given time, sunlight, and fertile soil, you will get an orange tree. Not an apple, pear, or lemon tree, but a tree that can do nothing other than produce—surprise, surprise!—oranges.

You may be thinking about the ways you can apply God's will to your life. That's because God's Spirit has planted the seed of faith in your heart. Now He is moistening it with the living water of God's Word, warming it with His protection and care, and nurturing it with His presence. Given time, is it any surprise that you will start bearing the fruit of faith—goodness, kindness, patience, peace? If that orange seed you planted developed into a strong healthy tree and produced more good oranges every season, you'd be pleased but not astonished. The same is true with you. The increasingly abundant fruit of your faith is what God has been expecting all along!

Let the good seed that God has planted in you grow deep-rooted and strong. Don't worry about production—that's already been established by the one who planted the seed!

Faith is not a sense,
nor sight, nor reason,
but taking God at his Word.

ARTHUR BENONI EVANS

Shout Out

I'm not surprised that my faith is showing!

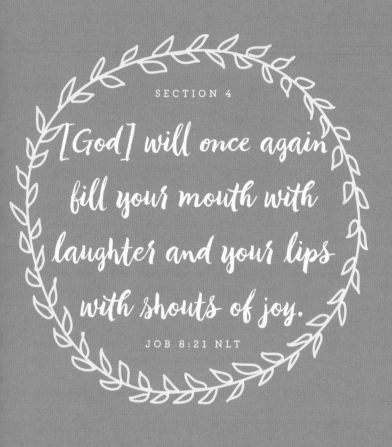

SECTION 4

[God] will once again
fill your mouth with
laughter and your lips
with shouts of joy.

JOB 8:21 NLT

The Doctor Is In

Your light shall break forth like the morning,
your healing shall spring forth speedily,
and your righteousness shall go before you.

ISAIAH 58:8 NKJV

When you see your physician with an ailment, you describe your symptoms in detail. What you're looking for isn't a cover-up for the symptoms, but a cure for whatever is causing your discomfort.

When it comes to spiritual discomfort, however, we often reach for something that will merely cover up the symptoms. For the telltale symptom of a nagging conscience, we might persuade ourselves that what we did wasn't so bad. Say the signs of spiritual sluggishness appear, and we decide we're too busy and we'll get back to God later. Or things are a mess right now, but as soon as we get our life back in order, we'll resume our spiritual journey. Isn't that like saying we'll go to the doctor when we get well? The time for a visit is now!

God, your Great Physician, wants you to come to Him whenever you sense that there's something wrong. Feelings of doubt, hopelessness, unhappiness, discontent? These are symptoms of spiritual distress. Why let them fester and get worse? You don't even have to call for an appointment! Your Great Physician is always available. Talk to Him immediately.

Spirituality really means:
"Holy Spirit at work."

LEON JOSEPH SUENENS

Shout Out

I will take care of my spiritual health!

Playing by the Rules

Teach me good judgment and knowledge,
for I believe Your commandments.
PSALM 119:66 NKJV

For fans of team sports, there's nothing like a keenly competitive game. Each team pits its skill, endurance, strength, and strategy against that of the other for a rousing match and a trophy for the winning side. Yet if fans can see that players are cheating, where's the thrill? It's no longer a contest, but a free-for-all. Cheating is a game changer!

Life, too, has rules. Just as societal rules work for our protection and well-being, God's rules advance our spiritual growth and enhance our enjoyment of living. The more consistently we apply His guidelines to our everyday thinking and behavior, the deeper, richer, and smoother our interactions with others. Gossip, intolerance, and spitefulness are game changers! The more conscientiously we choose God's ways instead of our own, the more satisfaction and fulfillment we discover. Pride, selfishness, discontent, and ingratitude are game changers!

While cheating players may find themselves pelted by half-eaten hot dogs and soda cups, the only thing God has to "throw" at you is forgiveness. If you want to bone up on your Coach's guidelines, reflect on His words in Scripture. Take His rules to heart, because they're at the heart of a life well lived.

I am sorry for the men who do not read the Bible every day. I wonder why they deprive themselves of the strength and the pleasure.

WOODROW WILSON

Shout Out

I will play by the rules—God's rules!

It's Due

I thank my God upon every remembrance of you.
PHILIPPIANS 1:3 NKJV

Don't you love someone who gives credit where credit is due? Especially when the credit is due to you! But as you gratefully acknowledge personal recognition, you also call attention to those who worked with you, because you know it couldn't have happened without them.

When you receive thanks and praise for the good you do, does the thanks and praise stop there? If so, you might be missing a valuable opportunity to give credit where credit is due—to others, and most of all to God's Spirit who enables and empowers you to accomplish His work in the world. He initiated your desire to grow in genuine love and make this love real in your everyday relationships. At the first, He stirred your heart to follow in His way, and to speak and act not for personal applause and self-celebration, but to faithfully and joyfully carry out His plan for your life.

The next time someone commends you for your helpfulness, generosity, patience, selflessness, or positive attitude, thank them, and then give credit where credit is due. It's by the grace of God that you are privileged to act as His hands and heart wherever you are!

*Most of the shadows of this life
are caused by standing
in one's own sunshine.*

RALPH WALDO EMERSON

Shout Out

I will give God the credit!

You're Worth It

Keep your lives free from the love of money,
and be satisfied with what you have.

HEBREWS 13:5 GNT

Periodically, you might go over your financials and figure out how much you're worth. After adding your assets and subtracting your debts, the bottom line will tell you if you're ready to buy a bigger house or invest a high percentage of income in your retirement fund. But the bottom-line number—six figures or two digits or next to a minus sign—is less important than your response to it.

God's gift of money is meant to be exactly that: a gift. As would any gift giver, He intends for you to enjoy it and use it for your well-being and the well-being of others. The larger the gift, however, the more responsibility you have to thank Him and share generously, remembering from whom your wealth has come. But even when money is short, that too is a gift. In it, God invites you to thank Him still, to spend, save, and share wisely, and to rely on Him to meet your needs.

In God's eyes, you're worth infinitely more than you can imagine. You possess His love, regardless of what your bank account looks like. You have His whole heart, and that's something no amount of money can buy.

*No man can tell whether
he is rich or poor by turning
to his ledger.
It is the heart which makes
a man rich.*

HENRY WARD BEECHER

Shout Out

I have what money can't buy!

More Than a Feeling

O give thanks to the Lord, for he is good,
for his steadfast love endures forever.

PSALM 136:1 NRSV

The minister, a dynamic speaker, holds his listeners spellbound. Then she pauses, looks at the audience, and shouts, "Can't you feel His love in this room?" With everyone else, you yell, "Yes!" but your heart says, "Not really." Or a friend, coping with a difficult situation, shares the latest developments. She looks at you and says, "But His love surrounds me. Don't you feel that way?" You nod and smile, fearful to confess that actually, you don't.

Love between two people in an intimate relationship expresses itself in many ways. Some, especially young lovers, may experience the thrill of ecstatic emotions and dreamy moods. But maturity teaches that the best, most long-lasting love, is a love not dependent on feelings, but is marked by commitment, understanding, forgiveness, humor, patience, and acceptance. They don't have to feel love to know that it's there. They don't have to go after emotion when they realize that they have something far more convincing. They have objective proof of love in actions.

Long ago, Jesus proved God's love by giving His life for your sake. He now lives to continue loving you. Feel it? Maybe. Know it? Yes!

This is the God we adore,
our faithful,
unchangeable friend,
whose love is as great
as his power, and neither knows
measure nor end.

JOSEPH HART

Shout Out

I love God's kind of love!

Seeing Is Believing

We will know for sure, by our actions,
that we are on God's side,
and our consciences will be clear.

1 JOHN 3:19 TLB

Imagine yourself listening to someone going on and on about his various awards and trophies. You might chuckle to yourself at his inflated sense of self-importance, but not when you know there's a wide gap between the fact and what he's saying. Now you feel sorry for him, because he thinks he's someone he observably isn't.

Sometimes those who say they are God-followers are like this self-satisfied fellow. They congratulate themselves on having made a confession of faith, or attending church regularly, or reading Scripture faithfully. A fine start, for sure, but what good is it if it's making no visible difference in their day-to-day behavior? Unpracticed faith finds no opportunity to prove itself in the real world. Nor can hidden belief work to change one life, much less the lives of others.

Let what you believe show in how you speak and act. Whenever you get some flak for your honesty or someone smirks at your values, it's a good sign that your faith is out there in the open and observable to all!

Faith wears ordinary clothes and proves herself in ordinary situations..

BERTHA MUNRO

Shout Out

If I believe it, I'm not afraid to show it!

A Godly Example

*He [God] sends rain for the ones who do right
and for the ones who do wrong.*

MATTHEW 5:45 CEV

Rose bushes brimming with prize-winning blooms thrive alongside pop-up clutches of dandelions. Peacocks, framed by glorious fans of iridescent feathers, strut their stuff while common sparrows flit from branch to branch in trees high above them. Both get the same sunshine and rain, spring breezes and winter winds. Nature doesn't discriminate!

Among your friends and acquaintances, there are probably quite a few who profess no belief in God, and yet are doing quite well. Maybe even better than you are. And what about pundits who publicly ridicule believers, or researchers who work hard to disprove Bible facts, or people you know who pepper every conversation with God's name? Their grass gets rain the same as yours—and you might even think it's greener!

God invites you to follow Him in loving all people, whether or not they love you back. He shows kindness and compassion toward His friends and to His enemies, as well. Every day, He provides food and shelter, health and wealth for nonbelievers and believers. But as for you, you have the joy and privilege of knowing whom to thank for it all!

*Nothing can make a man
truly great
but being truly good
and partaking in God's holiness.*

MATTHEW HENRY

Shout Out

I will follow Your example of love!

No Small Change

*Sometimes it takes a painful experience
to make us change our ways.*
PROVERBS 20:30 GNT

Change isn't always easy to take, except when the cashier owes it to us! Otherwise, change usually happens at inopportune times (as if there's a convenient time for our lives to be completely upended). Or when we really wouldn't mind something different coming along, the change that actually takes place isn't exactly what we would have chosen.

How you handle unexpected, especially unwelcome, change says a lot about your flexibility and your faith. Say you refuse to adapt to a new reality, so you fight it. Where is your energy being spent? On a futile battle! You end up drained, angry, and not at all prepared to see anything good in your new situation—or admit it if you do. Contrast that with faith that trusts God's wisdom. Now you might ask Him for His strength and guidance. You might pray for a spirit of acceptance and eyes to discern His will. Now there's a major change in perspective!

Many changes take place that are far beyond your control. You can fight them, or you can lean on God to show you His way ahead.

Change is the nursery of music,
joy, life, and eternity.

JOHN DONNE

Shout Out

Guide me, Lord, and show me
Your perfect way!

It's Okay to Laugh

God will yet fill your mouth with laughter and your lips with shouts of joy.

JOB 8:21 NCV

Is laughter an integral part of your daily life? You may be one of those people who is able to laugh in any and all situations. But you might also be someone who thinks that smiles and laughter in the face of world events and personal hardships and challenges is inappropriate.

If you are the latter, consider this. God encourages His followers to embrace a happy frame of mind, a relaxed and peaceful attitude, and yes, laughter. He has also given us some very good reasons why! First, because God is a God of forgiveness. As He lifts the weight of guilt from our hearts, we can live lightheartedly both spiritually and emotionally. Second, because God is a God of joy. He has power over all things, and ultimately joy will get the last laugh. And third, because God is a God of love. The kind of love that conquers fear and overcomes despair. The kind of love that laughs because it can.

You can know full well what's going on in the world and within you, and yet still believe, still hope, still smile, still laugh.

Always laugh when you can,
it is cheap medicine.

LORD BYRON

Shout Out

He frees the laughter in me!

Silent Struggles

When others are happy, be happy with them.
If they are sad, share their sorrow.

ROMANS 12:15 TLB

Most of us experience our share of life's ups and downs, but few of us will face extreme, headline-making struggles. Nonetheless, our personal struggles are real, and often they are known to no one but ourselves.

Never underestimate the seriousness of those things that test you every day. They are powerful enough to drag you down into despair and strong enough to pull you away from God. If you minimize them (because what you're going through isn't as awful as what someone else is going through), you are denying your own pain. In denying your pain, you never ask for, or receive, the comfort and healing that God has in store for you. If you complain about them (because you want everyone to know how much you suffer), you're sure to increase your troubles and decrease your welcome among others!

Day-to-day struggles aren't meant to be silent struggles. Pray for strength and patience, endurance and compassion. You aren't the only one. Ask God to lead you to those who can empathize with you, and those to whom (because of their struggles!) can offer a word of encouragement.

The friend in my adversity,
I shall always cherish most.

ULYSSES S. GRANT

Shout Out

I rely on You to help me through!

A Good Direction to Go

Pray much for others; plead for God's mercy upon them; give thanks for all he is going to do for them.

MATTHEW 5:45 CEV

How many of us have headed to a place we've never been before, yet thought we had the area all figured out? No need to get out the map! Our hotel is "just across the river," or "right up the next block," or "over there—pretty sure that's it!" Our confusion is understandable because it's our first time to go there, but why were we so reluctant to get directions?

We're sometimes like that in our spiritual journey. The landmarks are familiar enough to those of us who have been on the road a while, so we feel okay about putting away our map, the Bible. But then suddenly we realize that the territory is looking less and less the way we thought it would. We never expected to find ourselves in the middle of a broken family, facing a serious health issue, being asked to take on such an onerous responsibility. Now where did we put those directions?

Scripture, along with the thoughts of mature Christians who study it and reflect on it, are your road maps wherever you are on your life's journey. Read, hear, and listen. And never be afraid to ask for directions!

Abraham did not know the way,
but he knew the guide.

LEE ROBERSON

Shout Out

I'm going in the right direction!

Let It Pour!

Forgive us our sins, as we have forgiven those who sin against us.
MATTHEW 6:12 NLT

As winter snows slowly melt, the streets turn into lanes of muddy slush. Once graceful drifts become puddles, and once-lacy icicles tumble from house eaves and fence railings. The whole messy scene awaits the arrival of a warm spring rain to clear away the last traces of winter and prepare the world to bloom again!

Animosity, bitterness, and resentment are the cold, wet snows that can blanket our relationships. While we may maintain outward civility toward each other, our hearts are chilly and our true feelings are anything but pristine. Genuine forgiveness is like a warm spring rain. It loosens the ice, washes away the slush, and cleanses our hearts to make them ready for growth again. Growth in understanding, humility, generosity, and wisdom. Growth in a relationship that's ready to bloom again, this time fuller, stronger, healthier, and more vibrant than ever before.

If there's a layer of cold feelings dotting the landscape of your relationships, be the one to bring on the cleansing rains of forgiveness. And if you're looking for forgiveness from God your heavenly Father, expect a veritable downpour!

When you forgive
you in no way change the past—
but you sure do change
the future.

BERNARD MELTZER

As I am forgiven, so I forgive!

It's Really You!

You died to this life, and your real life is hidden with Christ in God.

COLOSSIANS 3:3 NLT

Few of us feel good coming across as someone we're not. While we might believe we need to pad the résumé to get the job, or exaggerate our accomplishments to impress our friends, a knot in the stomach reminds us that we're being less than truthful. We'd rather live authentically, in sync with our real selves.

So who are we, anyway? In the Bible, God tells us that He created us love to Him and serve others. Although humankind's original holiness has crumbled under the onslaught of sin, His Spirit working within us begins the work of turning our hardened hearts to soft, gentle, and yielding hearts. Hearts consumed with self to hearts enamored with Him. Hearts fearful of appearing weak and vulnerable to hearts that know true strength and confidence come from Him.

Your feelings do not describe the real you, but God does. The words He uses include beloved, blessed, forgiven, cherished, called to faith, and forever loved by Him. If you want to know who you really are, immerse yourself in His words. If you want to be in sync with your authentic self, live in Him.

It is only with the heart that one can see rightly; what is essential is invisible to the eye.

ANTOINE DE SAINT-EXUPERY

Shout Out

It's really me—and I am loved!

What's It About?

*He gives power to the weak, and to those
who have no might He increases strength.*

ISAIAH 40:29 NKJV

When you're determined to put your everyday
thoughts, words, and actions more in line with God's guidelines, you might think it's all about you. Suddenly you're
weighed down with musts and shoulds, have-to's and ought
to's, tension and pressure, struggles and strain. Whew!
You're overwhelmed before you even start!

Although living a spiritual life is about you, the
power to do it isn't up to you. It's not up to you to muster
enough force to resist old habits, or fend off temptation, or
make God-pleasing choices, or advance in spiritual wisdom
and understanding. That's God's domain! He knows you
can't do it by yourself, and He alone can enable you to follow Him. No human resolve can make it happen, much less
keep it going. No earthly know-how can comfort a guilt-
ridden heart, lift the eyes of a hurting soul, and transform
a way of burdens and darkness to a life of lightness and joy.

Your walk with God is all about you—but the
power to continue walking is all about God. That's
what makes it doable. That's what makes it joyful. Trust His
Spirit at work in you to supply everything you need along
the way!

Strength of my heart,
I rest in Thee,
fulfil Thy purposes
through me.

AMY CARMICHAEL

Shout Out

It's Your work in me that gets the job done!

The Blessing of Adversaries

Those also who render evil for good,
they are my adversaries,
because I follow what is good.

PSALM 38:20 NKJV

No doubt you're thankful for all of your friends. But how about those people who are, shall we say, less than friendly toward you? Maybe it's the intimidating boss, irritable neighbor, or controlling relative. Perhaps there's someone who seems bent on making life difficult for you. You might want to thank God for that person, too!

The boor who pokes fun at your appearance or background reveals how much self-confidence you possess. The mocker who ridicules your beliefs and values compels you t0 examine them to see if you think they're worth defending. The manipulator who tries to take advantage of you forces you to decide where your boundaries are. Those who don't come through for you teach you how to cope with disappointment, and those who lie to you strengthen your determination to keep your word. And that annoying grump you see every day? You get it when it comes to wearing a smile!

How would anyone—including you—realize how forgiving, compassionate, and understanding you are without a few in-your-face people to prove it? There are a lot of good things you know about yourself, thanks to those less-then-friendly "friends"!

He who wrestles with us strengthens our nerves, and sharpens our skill.

EDMUND BURKE

Shout Out

I forgive—and give thanks!

What's Up with That?

*We have courage in God's presence,
because we are sure that he hears us if we ask him
for anything that is according to his will.*

1 JOHN 5:14 GNT

A demanding child's outstretched hand might not get the candy. An obstinate adult's command may be met with complete indifference. Yet God invites us to shout, "I want *that!*" and know He's going to give it to us. So what's *that?*

That is anything we ask for that matches His good will for us. The more intensely we come to trust His wisdom and rely on His judgment, the less we're going to desire anything outside of His will. And while we're not certain of God's will when it comes to personal possessions or the outcome of life situations, we are most certain that He wants us to receive spiritual gifts. When *that* is deeper faith, stronger commitment, more vibrant joy, more embracing love, and a living relationship with Him, we can expect to get it. He desires our growth in kindness and compassion toward others, so we can ask and know, without doubting, that He will say *yes.*

You can point to faith, goodness, wisdom, inner peace, and say, "I want *that!*" and you've got it. You can ask for His good will to take place in your life with complete confidence. It *will* be done!

*We do not pray in order
to change his will,
but to bring our wills
into harmony with his.*

SIR WILLIAM TEMPLE

Shout Out

*I want nothing less than
Your perfect will for my life!*

Take Your Place

He brought me to his banquet hall
and raised the banner of love over me.
SONG OF SOLOMON 2:4 GNT

When you attend a dinner party, chances are you're sitting among people who belong to your social circle. Perhaps you've known one another for years and share many of the same memories. Or you're joined by a mutual interest in gourmet cooking or parasailing. Or the group belongs to the same organization or church.

Scripture frequently uses the image of a banquet table to tell us about God's family. We might be surprised, however, at the extent of His guest list! We might be astonished to recognize the former addict and convicted criminal sitting across the table from us. It's hard for us to fathom why the person who we believe willfully and maliciously causes so much havoc in our lives is placed next to us. We bristle as we scan faces so not like ours all around our heavenly Father's banquet table. What do we have in common with these people? Nothing short of God's great love for all of His children.

Through His Son Jesus, you are invited. By faith in Him, you have a place at His table. Come and eat!

*Faith finds food in famine
and a table in the wilderness.*

ROBERT CECIL

Shout Out

My place is assured!

Let's Face It

Happy are the people whose God is the Lord.
PSALM 144:15 NRSV

When we talk about "facing reality," the topic invariably revolves around life's tough truths. Sadness, despair, disappointment, loneliness, loss—yes, that's certainly one side of reality. But why are we so resistant to facing the sunny side of reality?

The splendor of God's creation is reality—it's all around us! So too is the wonder of the human body and mind, heart and soul. Nor can we ignore the real miracle of our very existence. Every day, we receive real blessings, both spiritual and material. We experience real love, joy, kindness, forgiveness, and compassion, and yet we're more apt to discuss their opposites at great length. We know there's nothing more real than courage that overcomes fear, resilience that surmounts hardship, faith that transcends doubt, and generosity that eases life's burdens for others.

If you're facing an unpleasant reality right now, remember to look at the other side of the coin. There you'll see that God's love, help, and comfort are not only real, but far more lasting and powerful than any pain or loss. When it's time to face reality, turn your face to the sunny side!

*Everything can be taken
from a man but one thing
—to choose one's attitude in any
given set of circumstances.*

VIKTOR E. FRANKL

Shout Out

Reality is God's work in my life!

Use Every Day

*Since you are eager for spiritual gifts,
strive to excel in them for building up the church.*

1 CORINTHIANS 14:12 NRSV

You're saving it "for good"—that dazzling dress, designer scarf, pricey ring. But it hangs in the closet, remains folded in a drawer, sits in the jewelry box so long that by the time a "good" occasion arrives, you've forgotten you have them!

God's spiritual gifts are extraordinarily dazzling, custom-made for you, and absolutely priceless. And they're meant to be used right now! His gift of compassion, for instance. Why keep it tucked away until you're visiting a friend in the hospital when every day you meet people who long to talk to someone who understands and cares? Or His gift of listening—really listening. Sure, you use it when a loved one pours out her heart to you, but everyone who speaks to you would appreciate having your undivided attention. Or His gift of helping. You readily pitch in when the call goes out for people to come to the rescue, but do you notice when a loved one could use a hand with day-to-day tasks?

God's gifts are the best gifts you will ever receive. Don't put them away in a closet or drawer. Use them every day. Put them on. Wear them.

*The most important thing in life
is to live your life
for something more important
than your life.*

WILLIAM JAMES

Shout Out

These gifts are made for using!

True Source of Confidence

It is better to trust in the Lord
than to put confidence in man.

PSALM 118:8 NKJV

You know the fable of the tortoise and the hare. When the tortoise challenged the hare to a race, the hare boasted that he would win handily. He was so confident, in fact, that he opted for a nap while the tortoise plodded along—right across the finish line! While the fable points out that "slow and steady wins the race," it also has something to say about misplaced confidence.

When we look to ourselves for confidence, we may fall into the same trap that the hare did. So we're thinking we're smart, skilled, and all-around winners. We're probably pretty proud, too, and our overwhelming confidence is hiding our weaknesses. Or, looking into ourselves, we might see little reason for self-confidence. We lack the education or credentials of those around us. We're not as attractive, healthy, or quick-witted. Our lack of confidence blinds us to our strengths.

Rather than looking to yourself, find your confidence in God. Let your self-assurance rest on the love He has for you, the gifts He has given to you, and the good plans He has for your life. Win the race with humble, joyful, uplifting confidence in Him!

*Nothing can be done
without hope and confidence.*

HELEN KELLER

Shout Out

I find my confidence in You!

The Sound of His Voice

My child, pay attention to my words;
listen closely to what I say.

PROVERBS 4:20 NCV

In a noisy crowd, most of us can pick out the voice of our parent, spouse, or child. A mother, even though asleep, will wake up to the sound of her teenager coming home late at night. And many a video-watching office worker can detect the sound of the boss's footsteps coming from across the hall!

As God enlivens the ears of your spirit, His voice is unmistakable. Even though you're surrounded by the clamor of a busy, noisy, and demanding world, you will hear His words of peace come through. Say you're lonely or sad or feel ashamed, and your words come only as whispers in the night. Nevertheless, you will discern His tender words of assurance, forgiveness, and reconciliation. Suppose you'd like to live more openly and confidently as one of His own. Listen! His encouragement will come through, loud and clear!

God's ears are always fine-tuned to the sound of your voice. As you pray, ask Him to fine-tune your ears to the sweet sound of His comfort and correction, reassurance and understanding, forgiveness and love.

The voice of God
is a friendly voice.
No one need fear to listen to it
unless he has already made up
his mind to resist it.

A.W. TOZER

Shout Out

I will open my ears to You, Lord!

Your Fearless Future

The Lord protects me from all danger;
I will never be afraid.

PSALM 27:1 GNT

You probably don't have to think back too far in your memory to recall a time you felt keenly aware of God's protective presence. Perhaps it was that close call on the highway, or the surgery you dreaded, but came through with flying colors. Or the time your grief overwhelmed you, but beneath it all, you found a place of heart-deep peace and rest.

Although God is with you always, you are likely to perceive Him more intensely when you're fearful, afraid, lonely, struggling, or grieving. Yes, scary, perilous, and troubling times come! But God makes them work for you, not against you. He uses them to draw you closer to Him, deepen your trust in Him, and strengthen your relationship with Him. The more you discern His presence in difficult times, the less you'll worry about them happening. Your past experience convinces you that just as He was there for you then, He will be there for you now and in the future.

What have you to fear? When you are close to Him, deeply trusting in Him, and sure of your relationship with him—absolutely nothing!

*All I have seen teaches me
to trust the Creator
for all I have not seen.*

RALPH W. EMERSON

Shout Out

I will face the future without fear!

When God Says Yes

People cast lots to learn God's will,
but God himself determines the answer.
PROVERBS 16:33 GNT

We often perceive God as a God of *no*—*no* to living for ourselves alone, *no* to putting our wants and needs first, *no* to doing whatever we feel like doing. So we say *no* to God, failing to stick around long enough to hear His divine, loving, and embracing *yes!*

He says *yes* to obedience and self-control so you can more fully focus on and enjoy all the good and lasting things that life has to offer. He says *yes* to your desire to grow in spiritual knowledge and discover more about His plans for you. He says *yes* to serving others because it's a pathway to joy, satisfaction, and fulfillment. When He tells you *no*, it isn't to limit you, but to guide you to His *yes*. It isn't intended to take away your freedom, but rather to make you free to find meaning, purpose, and genuine joy at every stage in life.

If you think your heavenly Father is more *no* than *yes*, sit with Him awhile. After you talk about all the *no's* you're hearing, be silent and let Him talk to you about all the *yesses* He has for you. Yes!

When we are obedient,
God guides our steps
and our stops.

CORRIE TEN BOOM

Shout Out

I will say Yes to God!

Bigger and Better

Your constant love is my guide;
your faithfulness always leads me

PSALM 26:3 GNT

Have you ever thrown your hands in the air and given up? Most of us have at some point! There's the bright idea that dimmed considerably once we started pursuing it. The perfect solution that wasn't quite as doable as we had imagined. The skill we thought we'd easily pick up, but required more time and effort than we were prepared to spend on it. So we abandoned these efforts and went on to bigger and better things.

Would God ever do the same thing when it comes to loving us? He created humankind in perfect holiness, but we willfully and deliberately separated ourselves from Him. Our decisions and choices stray from His divine will for our lives. The natural joy we could have had possessed is possible now only through His work in us. If we were in God's place, we would have given up long ago! We'd create something bigger, something better! But His love compels His continued commitment to us, and He will never give up on us.

God will never give up on you, and He's not put off by whatever shadows have crossed your heart. There's nothing bigger, nothing better, than His love for you!

With time and patience the mulberry leaf becomes satin.

CHINESE PROVERB

Shout Out

I am loved, and that will never change!

LIVE YOUR FAITH

Dear Friend,

This book was prayerfully crafted with you, the reader, in mind—every word, every sentence, every page—was thoughtfully written, designed, and packaged to encourage you...right where you are this very moment. At DaySpring, our vision is to see every person experience the life-changing message of God's love. So, as we worked through rough drafts, design changes, edits and details, we prayed for you to deeply experience His unfailing love, indescribable peace, and pure joy. It is our sincere hope that through these Truth-filled pages your heart will be blessed, knowing that God cares about you—your desires and disappointments, your challenges and dreams.

He knows. He cares. He loves you unconditionally.

BLESSINGS!
THE DAYSPRING BOOK TEAM

Additional copies of this book and
other DaySpring titles can be purchased
at fine bookstores everywhere.
Order online at dayspring.com
or
by phone at 1-877-751-4347